Conspiranoia
The Betrayed States of America

Daniel Pinchbeck

CONSPIRANOIA

CONTENTS

1 INTRODUCTION

In what follows, I intend to provide an overarching interpretation of current events. My goal is to resolve many conflicting narratives and conspiracy theories by proposing an encompassing framework. I am definitely not claiming what I propose here is the "absolute truth." We may never, in fact, know "the truth." Perhaps there isn't even one single or monolithic truth. But we must keep inquiring. It is crucial for us to analyze different framings and possibilities about what is happening now, so we can respond coherently. In what follows, I will dive deep into the darkness, hoping to shine some light on our current situation and illuminate our future prospects.

My primary interests are not political or ecological, but mystical and occult. Through psychedelics and shamanism, I had many direct experiences of subtle or invisible worlds, of "other dimensions" orthogonally related to our own. Even so, I believe we must engage with our social, political, and material circumstance. This requires challenging ourselves intellectually while honing our critical thinking skills. Psychedelics can be amazing tools for creative thinking. They decondition and deprogram us from inherited beliefs and ideologies. But people need to be given a new way of looking at the world — a new imprint — which doesn't abandon science and reason but reintegrates our current knowledge within a more expansive paradigm.

Over the last decades, much of the spiritual community got lost in a narcissistic, self-centered haze. Spiritual seekers — meditators, yogis, neo-shamans, and festival-goers — seek to avoid the darker elements of our reality. They focus on the "law of manifestation," "the power of now," and the never-ending quest for personal healing and ecstatic states. One common belief is that "Our thoughts create our reality." People take this to mean that we shouldn't focus on negative outcomes or malevolent forces, because this will give them energy. In fact, we can't reject, deny, or run away from our shadow material or that of the collective psyche, as we will end up suppressing and projecting the shadow. Carl Jung wrote, "We don't become enlightened by imagining figures of light but by making the darkness conscious."

As all of our myths tell us, the shadow can only be dispelled when we choose to face it. The consciousness community needs to confront the planetary emergency, instead of trying to escape from it. We can approach this as our spiritual mission. We can even be grateful for it as an opportunity for authentic initiation.

Recently, a number of New Age thought leaders have started to espouse Right Wing conspiracy theories such as Qanon and Pizzagate. Deluding themselves with magical thinking, they argue that Trump is not a crook and a con man working with a transnational syndicate of lawless dictators and gangster oligarchs to impose Fascism in the US. Instead he is seen as a crusader who is dismantling an evil "cabal" or "Deep State." Nothing could be further from the truth. The new alliance between New Age spirituality and Right Wing Neo-Fascism is alarming. It represents a regression backward into the dark waters of the unconscious, as we saw with Fascism in the 1930s, which also made an alliance with the occultism and spiritualism of its time.

I consider it my mission, as a thinker and writer, to find coherence. These days, this is no easy task. I compulsively seek an overall understanding — one that encompasses not just what newspapers report, but many areas and subjects that fall outside of the establishment worldview or paradigm. The mainstream paradigm or conventional wisdom — whatever is commonly accepted by most people — is largely defined by our mass media and education system. Most people — including many of our establishment pundits and "intellectuals" — don't question much further than that.

Traditionally, the establishment media defines a limit or boundary around what can be explored, what can be allowed into discourse. Collective beliefs and myths are also defined by a rhetorical style, a rhythm and tone, that shapes people's relationship to various ideas and subjects. In other words, people are not only told what to accept as true or meaningful, but how they should respond to the information given to them.

This normative worldview, of course, evolves and changes over time. These days, it is changing faster than ever before. This is partly due to outsiders such as myself, who illuminate its defects and provide new avenues for understanding and sense-making. It is also the case that social media and the Internet are having a de-centering effect on our discourse, in negative and positive ways.

Over the last years, we are seeing a number of subjects that were previously considered very marginal and ridiculous taken seriously by the mainstream. These include subjects like psychedelics, UFOs, and conspiracy theories — all areas I explored in depth in my work, and continue to explore. We have plunged into a global crisis, ecologically and geopolitically. Crises provide openings for new ideas to enter into the mainstream, for new world views to form and crystallize.

Breaking Open the Head, my first book, came out in 2002. The subject of that book was the psychedelic experience; particularly the use of visionary entheogenic plants by indigenous cultures around the world. When I wrote it, psychedelics were seen as stupid and pointless, "toys of the hippie generation" according to The New York Times, and rejected by the establishment. By taking the subject seriously and repositioning it, Breaking Open the Head helped to change the cultural tone. It softened the establishment view of psychedelics, paving the way for the renaissance in scientific research and shamanic exploration we see today.

In my twenties, I worked as a journalist and magazine editor in New York City. In my peer group, there was zero interest in mysticism or shamanism. Almost everybody shared the same scientific materialist, deeply cynical worldview. In fact, if you didn't share that viewpoint, you were ostracized. You couldn't get published in the glossy magazines that paid well and built your reputation.

While researching *Breaking Open the Head*, I had a series of earth-shattering, transformative visionary, psychic and paranormal episodes. As I overcame my own skepticism, I realized that the reductive materialist worldview, which sees consciousness as an epiphenomenon of brain activity, was incomplete. Although I started out as a materialist, I discovered there were other forces, other forms of consciousness, interacting with us. Psychic phenomena such as telepathy, synchronicity, along with many other psychic and occult powers: These are not folktales. Anyone can experience these things directly if they choose to investigate for themselves.

Indigenous cultures preserve knowledge of the esoteric and occult aspects of the world — of the "nature of reality" — that modern civilization forfeited. Because of this, we must take their wisdom seriously, despite the difficulty in translating from such different ways of thinking and knowing. My second book, *2012: The Return of Quetzalcoatl*, looked at the prophetic, mythological understanding that many ancient and indigenous cultures hold about this time. I linked these prophetic streams with ideas from Western philosophy and science, with rapid technological innovation and the climate crisis, as well as modern occult movements.

Books, much like people, take unique, idiosyncratic pathways through the world. While *Breaking Open the Head* was never a massive hit, it continues to sell steadily. *2012: The Return of Quetzalcoatl* became a New York Times bestseller when it was released in 2006. But later vanished from the collective consciousness. Back then, I was the subject of a disparaging feature in *Rolling Stone* and interviewed by Stephen Colbert on late-night television, where I introduced ayahuasca to the mass audience.

I never stated that anything drastic or amazing would happen at the end of the year 2012. Even so, I was later ridiculed in *The New York Times* and elsewhere as a "doomsday thinker," a failed prophet. In fact, the essential projections I made in that book, following the wisdom of many indigenous and ancient cultures, seem even more true today. It does seem to be the case that we are undergoing an accelerated transformation, impacting the physical Earth and human consciousness. Those insights still need to be understood properly and integrated in relationship to the time we are in now. *2012: The Return of Quetzalcoatl* remains a useful guide, a key for those who want to understand what's happening philosophically and metaphysically, but also individually and through our direct experience.

As a result of accepting the validity of taboo areas like psychic phenomena, crop circles, mysticism, and shamanism, I lost my access to mainstream media outlets. I was no longer able to write for *The New York Times Magazine* or get my books published through major US publishers. In some ways, I contributed to my own ostracism — but that is another story.

There are benefits to being an outsider. I don't feel beholden to any societal pressures, or any need to conform in any direction. When I make mistakes, I admit and address them. I have the freedom to think and write what I want.

Writing my first book, I learned that the establishment — rejecting, due to its crude scientism, any possibility of psychic experience, denying any concept of a soul or a spirit or any dimension of being beyond the material — was wrong about the most fundamental aspects of reality. After that, I realized I couldn't trust the establishment view in many areas. Many friends in Manhattan climbed the ladder of success. They graduated from Ivy League schools. They attained prestigious positions in *The New Yorker* or *The New York Times*, or made it as investment bankers, fine artists, lawyers, or film producers. They were hyper-intelligent, quick witted, cunning. Yet I found they lacked a more encompassing wisdom. They were shut off to new ideas or divergent thinking that might threaten their worldview.

You find success in our society by fitting into the establishment. Ivy League schools, for the most part, don't teach students how to think freely but how to ace tests and win status competitions. The "best and brightest" are trained to maximize their personal advantage within elite hierarchies of power and privilege. Thinking creatively, or acting courageously according to principle, does not get you ahead, for the most part. Siding with the authorities, kowtowing to wealth and power, does.

Generally, we are rewarded for gaining expertise in particular narrow fields, not for exercising our innate ability for comprehensive, systemic thinking. In the 1960s, the design scientist Buckminster Fuller saw that our society was forcing people to hyper-specialize in their particular disciplines. He warned this was dangerous for our future. We needed to become generalists again so we could bring together insights from different domains to make better decisions. In my work, I have taken Fuller's idea to heart, developing my perspective as a generalist, synthesist, and systems thinker.

One theme of my work for twenty years has been the ecological emergency: The overwhelming crisis of climate change, species extinction, and atmospheric pollution that threatens our survival as a species. My first book on psychedelic shamanism started out as a response to the ecological crisis. In the late 1990s, I wrote articles about environmental issues for *Esquire* and other magazines. I was shocked by the magnitude of what was happening to our planet, and how the media under-reported it. I quickly found that most people either didn't care or couldn't pay attention. They lacked the bandwidth if it didn't directly impact their career path.

When I tried to understand why we didn't care as we should, I realized this detachment and disconnection was directly linked to the grim materialist worldview, which we had internalized. I saw how all of us — my peers and I — were trapped by this belief in scientific materialism. Since consciousness was only accidental, an epiphenomenon of the brain, our lives lacked for greater meaning or purpose. We assumed that death was obliteration, annihilation. This materialist paradigm was like an air-tight prison that allowed no escape.

Scientific materialism is inherently nihilistic. To save humanity from ecological Armageddon (if that is still possible), we need a species-wide drive toward self-limitation. We will only be able to fight for wide-ranging, systemic changes when people agree that there is an inherent value in human existence as well as a transcendent dimension, beyond space and time. We must find the passion to fight for what's right, even when it goes against our short-term, immediate self-interest.

Another major theme of my work is initiation. For ancient and indigenous cultures around the world, the purpose of initiation is to directly access other levels of transcendent and transpersonal consciousness. Initiation is like a conscious, temporary death: You die to the ego-ic mind and awaken to the astral and spiritual realms. This is why the ancient Hermetic tradition tells us: *"Die before you die."* Similarly, the Gnostic Christ in The Gospel of Thomas says: *"Open the door for yourself so you will know what is."* I believe that our transitory lives only make sense when we discover for ourselves, with some degree of certainty, that a part of us continues after death. By undergoing initiation, by accessing these other dimensions of reality, you permanently transform your relationship to reality.

Before I explored psychedelic shamanism, I believed in the reductive materialist worldview. I had been indoctrinated into it by my parents, the media, my peers, teachers at school. I was in the depths of an existential crisis in my late twenties when I asked myself: How did I know it was true? I realized I didn't know it for a fact. All of my information was secondhand, received from outside sources.

My psychedelic trips from college remained indelibly etched in my memory. They suggested there might be something else — other dimensions of consciousness, invisible regions of being, to be excavated. I decided I would explore psychedelics again, to see if they revealed a doorway out of the materialist prison. I started writing about them for magazines. I was amazed by what I found through my own journeys.

I still believe that only a new revelation — a new approach to reality — can ignite a transformational movement with the power to address the biospheric crisis we have unleashed. In *How Soon Is Now?* (2017), I integrated insights from years of psychedelic trips to put together a pragmatic solution-based approach to the ecological emergency. I proposed the changes we need to make to our technical systems (agriculture, energy, industry, and so on) as well as our social systems (government and economy). I considered how we could deliberately engineer a transformation of the collective consciousness using mass media and social networks. If we don't manage this, it seems clear we will see a catastrophic collapse of global civilization in the next decades, certainly costing billions of lives and probably leading to human extinction.

I naively believed *How Soon Is Now?* was the wake up call the world was waiting for. Unfortunately, my book came out just after Donald Trump's 2016 election. At that point, there was no way to get people excited about prospects that seemed so distant from their immediate concerns.

Since then — like all of us — I have been witnessing ongoing events, living through them, while thinking about what it all means, and what is to come. I maintain a metaphysical, occult perspective on what's happening. As I defined it in *2012: The Return of Quetzalcoatl*, my esoteric understanding synthesizes concepts from Carl Jung, Rudolf Steiner, Gurdjieff, Eastern religions, indigenous cultures, and other sources. I look at the procession of historical events as part of a greater archetypal, mytho-poetical process — a cosmic story in which we are embedded.

Since 2012, it feels like we have pierced through the veil, in some strange inchoate way. Time seems to be unfolding as if it were no longer exactly "real;" many of us feel like we are in a dystopian movie or video game. It is as if we have already crossed over to the other side somehow, living through a mythological projection from the collective unconscious; a fever dream, or perhaps a nightmare, that some restless, tormented god, devil, or Archon is having.

As I will discuss at the end, the occult understanding provides a framework that makes all of this sensible, in a way that increasingly meshes with the scientific worldview. Despite the social and environmental decay we see around us, there are good reasons for faith, hope, and action. But first, we must apply our critical thinking skills to claw our way to clarity.

We need a baseline of shared coherence, for reasons that will become clear in what follows. We must establish a comprehensive understanding, even if we cannot solve the riddle entirely. I personally think that this is not a spurious pursuit but a matter of life and death for us. Without agreement on what's happening to our world, we won't be able to safeguard what remains of our rights and freedoms or do what we can to preserve a human future on Earth.

2. THE CABAL

Conspiracy theories often posit the existence of a tiny cabal who seem to possess superhuman knowledge and forethought. It is presumed that this group acts as one, with deliberate intent and a well-formulated long-term plan. Many people want to believe that such a cabal exists, that its members are incredibly wicked and extremely intelligent — even Satanic.

According to the virally contagious conspiracy narrative called Qanon, the technocratic ruling elite is a sadistic cabal, addicted to pedophilia and child sacrifices, consuming a drug, Adrenochrome — originally popularized by Hunter S. Thompson in *Fear and Loathing in Las Vegas* — which they extract from the brains of sacrificed babies. While we will explore the roots of this theory later, it seems unlikely to be true. Whether it is a fantasy or a collective delusion or even a targeted PsyOp, we still need to understand why so many people find this particular narrative so compelling and mesmerizing at this time.

There isn't a single cabal controlling world affairs. Instead, a number of factions compete as well as cooperate at the apex of the pyramid of wealth and power. These factions interact with each other in complex ways. Sometimes they oppose or undercut each other. More often than not, they share enough of an agenda that they can work toward similar goals without explicitly coordinating their actions. I believe there is, also, an occult or esoteric component underlying world events, in which secret societies play a role. I will consider what that means and how it contributes later on.

Rather than one cabal, various factions make up the global "power elite." These groups bond over their arrogance, elitism, and entitlement (the "masters of the universe" mentality). Some of their members possess, also, psychopathic personality disorders.

It is well established that a small proportion of humans, perhaps one percent of the general population, are innately psychopathic. Others can be influenced or trained to behave in that way. People possessing psychopathic personality disorders tend to thrive in hierarchical corporate, military, and governmental structures. Because they have no ethical compunction when it comes to collateral damage or "externalities," they steadily rise to positions of power in systems based on domination and exploitation.

We can all sense many hidden layers and secret agendas crisscrossing beneath the surface of current events. Overall, when you try to comprehend what is underway and what is being perpetrated, you enter a dizzying labyrinth that induces cognitive dissonance. How did we end up with the bizarre fiasco of the Trump Presidency? How is it possible for governments to keep increasing the monetary supply beyond any historical precedent, without repercussions? Why does information about the

Coronavirus pandemic keep fluctuating? Instead of moving forward toward a better world with more humane values, why are we rapidly regressing and degenerating?

Why did the world react in such a chaotic way to the virus, potentially causing starvation on a vast scale? Inevitably, far more people will die from the residual effects of government action then will suffer from the virus itself. The UN estimates as many as 130 million people could starve due to the economic impacts, while one million have died from Covid at this point. The lives of hundreds of millions more have been ruined by the economic consequences. Considering the scenario planning done in advance, all of this was predictable. Yet little was done to address it.

We find ourselves in strange new territory. We are experiencing an ongoing collapse of coherence: A loss of signal and disintegration into noise. Fear and irrationality have taken hold of our social body as people seek for any sense of security or any stable sense of what the future may hold. This is impacting many of us very intimately and also rippling through society as a whole. We need to establish an understanding that encompasses all of the current trends and factors, so we can see and act clearly. Without that, we are lost.

3. THE DISUNITED STATES

Until recently seen as the great beacon of opportunity, wealth-creation, and innovation, the United States of America has been leading the global tailspin toward self-destruction over the last few years. There is a simplistic tendency among liberals and progressives to blame Donald Trump for this. But that is absurd. Deeper trends, hidden forces and factions, have undermined America, like termites gnawing away at its foundations. One could just as well blame the Clintons and Obama for this catastrophe. In the end, they are all symptoms of a deeper disease.

It is extraordinary that the situation in America has shifted so rapidly from a seemingly stable neoliberal democracy toward neo-Fascism, Mussolini-style corporatism, with the increasing possibility of full-scale military rule, suppression of dissidents, mass internment camps, and eventually (part of the pattern) genocides. This was the trend even before the Coronavirus pandemic left fifty million unemployed and helped incite the Black Lives Matter uprisings. We are seeing the results of systemic rot and corruption over a very long time.

We are discovering what happens when previously invisible processes, like underwater currents, break through to the surface. All of the structures we believed to be stable and secure had eroded over time. They were ready to fail.

What is breaking down is not only the government, the financial system, and the sense of social cohesion that holds our civilization together: It is the underlying ideology of technological civilization with its linear model of progress. America — and the "American Dream" of individual freedom and unlimited prosperity — expressed this ideology more than any country on Earth. The breakdown of this system could allow for something new to emerge over time: A new set of beliefs that integrate a deeper wisdom drawn from many traditions, including indigenous cultures rooted in ceremonial practices, initiatory techniques, and ecological stewardship. But we are very far from there right now.

For many decades, the US political system has offered its citizens an insulting choice between two similarly corrupt, compromised parties. As a child growing up in New York in the 1970s, I already felt that democracy in the USA was an engineered fraud. Beneath the paper-thin veneer of choice, our country was authoritarian; our much-vaunted democratic government a convenient pretext for ongoing corporate rule and the octopus-like extension of our global Empire. No matter who was President, our military continued to fight illicit wars while our intelligence agencies engineered coup d'états and assassinations.

There are many ways we can interpret our history to understand how our political system rigidified, going back to the country's foundations. Government is best understood as a continuously negotiated contract between the rulers — the governing elites — and the people. The American Revolution, the Declaration of Independence, and the Constitution were great advances, but flawed and imperfect. They established basic rights such as free speech, freedom of assembly, the right to vote and to bear arms, and proposed human equality as an ideal. This new social contract, modeled on Enlightenment principles, was a huge step forward from older forms of monarchy. The rights guaranteed to citizens in the US Constitution provided the model followed by modern constitutional governments around the world. These freedoms included "freedom to trade," which enabled the transition to Capitalism, the globalized economy we have today.

Capitalism evolves convulsively. It creates frequent crises that must be resolved, one way or another, through large-scale government interventions. For example, in the 1930s, the Great Depression led to the New Deal. American workers and their allies used collective pressure to force major concessions from the ruling elite who were frightened by the specter of revolutionary Communism.

America emerged victorious from World War Two, after overcoming its noninterventionist stance. As Europe lay in ruins, America took over the reigns of the global Empire developed over centuries of European imperialism and colonialism. After two devastating world wars, Europe had lost its gusto for further conquest. The US and its European allies continued to enhance their global power through financial and cultural as well as military means.

We maintained hegemony for more than a half century through the UN, World Bank, and other international bodies. During the Cold War, we fought against the spread of Russian and Chinese Communism. We overturned democratically elected Left Wing governments in Latin America, and supported dictatorships in the Middle East.

In the 1960s, Lyndon Johnson's Great Society initiative meant an increase in social programs, aid to the poor, and desegregation, requiring increased taxes on the wealthy. But something happened between the late 1960s and today: Social progress in the US came to a halt and started rolling backwards. Growth in real wages stagnated and declined. We went from a period where the majority of people had stable careers with guaranteed retirements, to a "gig economy" where the masses found themselves forced to compete for "bullshit jobs." Capital increasingly concentrated at the top of the financial pyramid. The middle class contracted while a tiny group became exponentially wealthier. We slipped back toward oligarchy.

We can identify a number of factors contributing to this rollback. As America took control of the global Empire, this led to a massive expansion of our military industrial complex, which increasingly pursued its own agenda. Capitalism continued to do what it does: Creating and then exploiting new markets, converting natural resources as well as previously uncommodified domains of human activity into profit centers and industries.

During the 1970s, the US shifted from an economy based on production to one based on consumption, as we outsourced industrial jobs to cheaper labor markets in Asia and Latin America. The power we possessed by holding the world's reserve currency allowed us to accelerate the shift from an economic model based on tangible goods to one that prioritized financial services. We went off the gold standard in the early 1970s, delinking the dollar from any tangible asset.

Built in 1973, the World Trade Towers (ironically, considering their fate) were like tuning forks, symbolizing the frequency shift to a virtual, financialized economy. The 1980s was the era of Wall Street, where vast fortunes were made through junk bonds, hedge funds, currency speculation, and suchlike. All of this wealth-creation was parasitic; producing nothing in itself, it fed off the capital produced by human labor. The financial elites, as they gained more power, were able to fix the system for their own benefit. After the 2008 financial crash, induced by corrupt practices by banks and investment firms, the Government bailed out the financial elites, while ignoring the mass population. This pattern repeated itself with the financial stimulus during the pandemic.

The Founding Fathers designed the US Government for a rapidly growing country of farmers, with a much smaller population, at a time when technological innovation happened much slower than it does today. While there was a great deal of genius and flexibility in its design, it became less and less adaptable over time. Today we are in a period of rapid changes, when new technologies can instantly transform how we communicate with each other, how financial instruments are traded, or cause a new, never-before seen threat to our immediate survival.

As good as it is, our government is based on 18th Century social technology. It needs to be upgraded for the world we have now. But we don't have any plan for how to do this. It is becoming obvious that the choice is either more democracy (direct democracy, local sovereignty) or none at all.

Our inherently parasitic and exploitative financial system, backed up by a massive military machine, overcame the restraints traditionally placed on it by the people, through our government. Technologies that could support human liberation, such as the Internet, were subverted to serve the corporate control agenda. We don't have a clear path to undo the damage that has been done. Unfortunately, this subversion takes place at a time when we need human solidarity and collective global action like never before, to confront the ecological emergency.

What is happening now is so enormous that it is difficult for our minds to grasp. This helps to explain the magnetic pull of simplistic conspiracy theories like Qanon. People sense that the veneer of logic and scientific rationality that provided the justification for technocratic society is cracking apart. But they lack the tools to think clearly about what is underway, as well as practical means to resist the downward direction in which we are now cascading. At the same time, our collective Psyche is under attack from highly sophisticated operations that use weaponized mass media and AI-assisted algorithms to exploit our psychological weaknesses. These forces of mind control seek to drag the world down into hell. They may well succeed.

I am writing this a few weeks before the 2020 US election. Trump's 2016 "election" was already, most probably, a partly engineered coup. It seems likely that

the voting machines in crucial swing states were
hacked electronically, as the final tally of votes
deviated significantly from reliable poll numbers. This
"election" was assisted not just by Russian hackers
but by elements in the intelligence agencies and their
proxies in the mainstream media.

The New York Times, for instance, focused single-
mindedly on the non-issue of Hilary's emails during
the election's crucial last days. Facebook was
manipulated by Cambridge Analytica, an intelligence
operation which built an AI-powered machine to
target voter's psychological weaknesses. While a few
courageous journalists like Jennifer Cohn and Greg
Palast cover the likelihood of electronic tampering,
the mainstream media continues to ignore the subject
altogether.

We know from the Congressional hearings on
Operation Mockingbird that the mainstream media is
infiltrated and its content is, to a certain extent,
overseen and controlled by US intelligence agencies.
It is widely believed that the US intelligence
community is largely against Trump. Obviously that is
not the case. We might ask ourselves instead: Why
would certain factions within the intelligence
community (integrated with the military and fossil
fuel industries) prefer Trump and want him to win?

There is at least one underlying purpose around
which many factions, including Russian and Chinese
interests and US Right Wing evangelicals, seem to
have converged: They desire to subvert and dismantle
the remaining institutions of American democracy.
This includes a government based on the Separation
of Powers, as well as the rights guaranteed to US
citizens in the Constitution. A number of these
factions saw Trump as a kind of battering ram who

would accelerate the dismantling of the liberal nation state with its Constitutional protections and citizen's rights. This is also why these forces are inciting Civil War and violence in the US: It provides an opportunity for increased dictatorial, oligarchic, and military rule — not just in the US, but globally.

The US system of government, as imperfect as it is, still ensures basic rights such as free speech, freedom of assembly, and the right to bear arms. These rights became the model or template for constitutional governments around the world. By sabotaging and dismantling this system of Constitutional protections within the US, these factions, which include authoritarian elements within the US and the leadership in countries with authoritarian regimes, are setting the stage for intensifying global despotism. China and Russia have long seen America as their primary adversary. They are effectively using "asymmetric warfare" tactics, such as virtual intelligence operations, to push the US toward breakdown.

Conspiracy theories tend to be simplistic. There are probably many levels or gradations between intentionally orchestrated conspiracies where every nuance is plotted out in advance, and opportunities that can be exploited. The military and intelligence community studies and anticipates many future scenarios as probable, possible, or inevitable. They prepare for what those scenarios offer both as crisis and opportunity.

Those controlling the levels of power from behind the scenes have contingency plans for how to use crises, when they occur, in order to advance their particular agenda or ideology, as Naomi Klein explored in *The Shock Doctrine*. When it occurs in the economic sphere, she called it "disaster capitalism." She found that financial and corporate interests intentionally capitalize on the worst crises and catastrophes. They use these crises to accomplish objectives which would meet with too much popular resistance in normal times.

This helps to explain past events like "9–11", another experience of collective cognitive dissonance (cognitive dissonance is an intentional tool used by the power elite, since a confused and scared populace is easily controlled). Many of those who study the evidence in depth conclude there must have been a conspiracy behind 9–11. There were too many anomalous, inexplicable aspects of it.

These anomalies include the way the Twin Towers collapsed straight down, indicating a controlled demolition; the small hole in the Pentagon which seemed to reveal it was struck by a targeted missile instead of a massive jet plane; the immediate recovery of the intact passports of the terrorists miles away from the impact; the collapse of Building Seven later that day; the fact that the terrorist pilots had been trained at a CIA-run flight school in Florida, and so on. However, it was never possible to find the "smoking gun." Establishment liberals and mainstream journalists pointed out that carrying out a conspiracy on such a vast scale would be unmanageable and impossible. This also seemed reasonable and hard to refute.

And yet, on the other hand, Vice President Dick Cheney and Secretary of State Donald Rumsfeld were part of Project for the New American Century (PNAC), a think tank that published a paper, a few years before Bush's election, stating that the US required a Pearl Harbor-level inciting incident in order to muster the popular will to use massive military force to access the strategic oil reserves of the Middle East. Although the terrorists had nothing to do with Iraq at all, 9–11 was used as pretext for a war in Iraq that resulted in the deaths of over a million Iraqi civilians and allowed US military forces to control that oil-rich country.

Immediately after 9–11, the Patriot Act was pushed through Congress. This was a significant strike against our Constitutional rights, which continue to be eroded now (for instance, due to the pandemic, we have lost freedom of assembly and intensive, ongoing surveillance is becoming commonplace). It was totally clear, at that time, that the Patriot Act had been prepared well in advance. Anticipating popular resistance, they waited to introduce it until the moment after a national emergency, with the compliant media amping-up collective fear over terrorism. The Department of Homeland Security (a name with sinister authoritarian undertones) was created at that time. It has never gone away.

We may never know exactly how "9–11" was architected and orchestrated. It may be the case that it was permitted to happen, actively aided and abetted, or entirely plotted out. Many have remarked on the peculiar synchronicity of the Gates-funded Event 201, which brought together experts to run a simulation of a global pandemic just a few months before Covid. Earlier planning for a future pandemic included the Dark Winter exercise[1], conducted by high level government officials in 2001. Dark Winter

---

[1] "America's Pandemic War Games Don't End Well: One simulation of an uncontrolled disease outbreak ended with riots and the Guard on the Streets," by Mark Perry; *Foreign Policy;* April, 2020

predicted this year's events with eerie accuracy, including shortages of basic medical supplies and the use of the National Guard to quell riots. We will speak more about Gates later. On the morning of 9/11, similarly, a number of military training exercises took place. These oddly timed exercises may have inhibited military response to the errant jet planes targeting the World Trade Centers.

Another problem in the United States is the powerful influence of evangelical Christianity, which has formed an alliance with the fossil fuel interests and Far Right Libertarians. The fanatic ideology of Christian Fundamentalism in the United States includes the firm belief that we are approaching the time of Apocalypse and Armageddon. These events must occur literally, as presented in The Revelation to John, before the believing faithful can ascend to Heaven, as described in the bestselling Left Behind novels. Evangelicals see Trump as part of their prophecy. Christian fanaticism exacerbates the dangers already present in the US, potentially leading to violent conflicts and civil strife, which many of the faithful would welcome as a sign that we are nearing the end times.

4. A DELICIOUS BOWL OF BAT SOUP

When the Coronavirus pandemic happened last March, the world went into panic mode. How can we understand the origin of this virus? Should we even bother to try to understand it? I believe that we need to do so — as understanding what happened may help prepare us for the next set of approaching future shocks. By gaining insight into the geopolitical dynamics currently underway, we might improve our future survival prospects.

Let's consider the options: The virus was either an accidental and random occurrence, spreading from a bowl of bat soup slurped down at the Wuhan wet market, or it was bio-engineered in a laboratory. If it was engineered, it was either released accidentally, or it was intentionally unleashed as a biological weapon. If it was intentionally released, this was either done by China alone, or there was international collusion behind it.

I believe we can satisfactorily address, at least, the question of whether Coronavirus-19 was manmade or natural. It seems almost certain that Coronavirus-19 was engineered in the Wuhan virology laboratory, despite the efforts of establishment scientists, writing in Nature Magazine and elsewhere, to claim otherwise. Scientists working in fields such as biotechnology have a lot to lose, in terms of funding as well as popular support, if it becomes commonly known that Covid was a Frankenstein monster. The level of collusion between the mainstream media and the pharmaceutical companies and biotechnology industry is extreme at this point. Pharmaceutical companies, as advertisers and sponsors, provide one of the mainstream media's largest revenue streams. As much as 70% of the revenues for Fox evening news programs, to take one example, come from pharmaceutical advertising.

The mainstream narrative of the origin of Coronavirus-19 involves cross-species transmission of the virus from a bat to a human at the Huanan Seafood Wholesale Market in Wuhan, China, a city of 11 million people, 650 miles from Beijing. What makes this story highly dubious is that Professor Zhengli Shi, the world's leading research scientist into exactly these types of coronaviruses, ran the Wuhan Institute of Virology, just a few miles away from the market where the transmission purportedly occurred. The Institute was "China's only P4-Level Biosafety Laboratory capable of storing, studying, or engineering Pathogen Level 4 microbes such as other coronaviruses, Ebola, Severe Acute Respiratory Syndrome, SARS, H5N1 influenza virus, Japanese encephalitis, and dengue."[2]

For years, Professor Shi — or "bat lady," as she is known — and her team have not just been studying,

---

[2] "Only one lab in China can safely handle the new coronavirus," by Nicoletta Lanese; *Live Science*; January 22, 2020

but actively creating, new, novel Coronaviruses from bats, tinkering with them so they can cross over to human populations more easily. This research has been partly funded by the US Government, which gave $7.5 million in grants to Shi's work at the Wuhan Virology Institute during 2014–2017. According to *The Diplomat*[3], the purpose of the grants "appears to have included work on "gain-of-function": research that investigates how a virus can gain the ability to infect a new type of animal." With hindsight, it is clear that this gain-of-function research should never have been done.

Shi was part of an international research team that took a Coronavirus from a horseshoe bat, combining it with material taken from HIV to make it more easily transmissible to humans. In a research paper co-authored by Shi, 'Difference in Receptor Usage between Severe Acute Respiratory Syndrome (SARS) Coronavirus and SARS-Like Coronavirus of Bat Origin' (2008)[4], the researchers describe how, in technical terms, they were seeking to engineer a bat coronavirus so it can be transmitted to humans:

"From crystal-structural analysis of the S-ACE2 complex, it was predicted that the S protein of SL-

---

[3] "Why Would the US Have Funded the Controversial Wuhan Lab? Reports about the connection between the U.S. National Institutes of Health and the Wuhan Institute of Virology risk feeding conspiracy theories about the origins of COVID-19;" by Justin Fendos; *The Diplomat*; May 13, 2020

[4] "Difference in Receptor Usage between Severe Acute Respiratory Syndrome (SARS) Coronavirus and SARS-Like Coronavirus of Bat Origin;" by Wuze Ren, Xiuxia Qu, Wendong Li, Zhenggang Han, Meng Yu, Peng Zhou, Shu-Yi Zhang, Lin-Fa Wang, Hongkui Deng, Zhengli Shi; Journal of Virology; 2008

CoV is unlikely to use huACE2 as an entry receptor, although this has never been experimentally proven due to the lack of live SL-CoV isolates. Whether it is possible to construct an ACE2-binding SL-CoV S protein by replacing the RBD with that from SARS-CoV S proteins is also unknown. In this study, a human immunodeficiency virus (HIV)-based pseudo-virus system was employed to address these issues. Our results indicated that the SL-CoV S protein is unable to use ACE2 proteins of different species for cell entry and that SARS-CoV S protein also failed to bind the ACE2 molecule of the horseshoe bat, Rhinolophus pearsonii. However, when the RBD of SL-CoV S was replaced with that from the SARS-CoV S, the hybrid S protein was able to use the huACE2 for cell entry, implying that the SL-CoV S proteins are structurally and functionally very similar to the SARS-CoV S. These results suggest that although the SL-CoVs discovered in bats so far are unlikely to infect humans using ACE2 as a receptor, it remains to be seen whether they are able to use other surface molecules of certain human cell types to gain entry. It is also conceivable that these viruses may become infectious to humans if they undergo N-terminal sequence variation, for example, through recombination with other CoVs, which in turn might lead to a productive interaction with ACE2 or other surface proteins on human cells."

The language is dense, but as one wades through it, the meaning becomes clear: The scientists in Wuhan "employed" "a human immunodeficiency virus (HIV)-based pseudovirus system" to make their novel coronavirus potentially transmissible to humans. Success!

Then eight years later, as *Nature Magazine* reported in 2015[5], Professor Shi's team investigated "a virus called SHC014, which is found in horseshoe bats in China… The researchers created a chimaeric virus, made up of a surface protein of SHC014 and the backbone of a SARS virus that had been adapted to grow in mice and to mimic human disease. The chimaera infected human airway cells — proving that the surface protein of SHC014 has the necessary structure to bind to a key receptor on the cells and to infect them." Success yet again!

The danger of Professor's Shi's gain of function research deeply concerned many virologists. Simon Wain-Hobson from the Pasteur Institute in Paris noted presciently, "If the virus escaped, nobody could predict the trajectory." Richard Ebright, a molecular biologist and biodefence expert at Rutgers University, fretted: "The only impact of this work is the creation, in a lab, of a new, non-natural risk." In fact, in 2014, the National Institute of Health in the US prohibited this kind of research. Then, in 2017, it permitted this research again[6]. It is telling that the mainstream media has done very little reporting on this.

Both the Chinese and American military are fascinated by the potential use of viruses and diseases as bioweapons. Recently, China has indulged in international espionage to gain a competitive edge. As

---

[5] "Engineered bat virus stirs debate over risky research: Lab-made coronavirus related to SARS can infect human cells;" by Declam Butler, *Nature* (2015)

[6] "US government lifts ban on risky pathogen research: The National Institutes of Health will again fund research that makes viruses more dangerous;" by Sarah Reardon; *Nature* (2017)

reported in many outlets[7], Canada exiled a group of leading Chinese virologists last July for sending samples of some of the world's most lethal diseases to Beijing: "Suspected of espionage for China, a group of Chinese virologists was forcibly evicted from the Canadian National Microbiology Laboratory (NML) in Winnipeg, where they had been running parts of the Special Pathogen Program of Canada's public health agency. One of the procedures conducted by the team was the infection of monkeys with the most lethal viruses found on Earth. Four months prior to the Chinese team's eviction, a shipment containing two exceptionally virulent viruses — Ebola and Nipah — was sent from the NML to China."

Despite the evidence that Professor Shi's laboratory in Wuhan was actively engineering novel Coronviruses from those found in bats, designed to be more easily transmittable to humans, incorporating elements from HIV and other sources, mainstream media in the West[8] maintains dogmatic faith in the narrative that Coronavirus-19 occurred accidentally via a cross-species transmission. As in many instances, we find the mass "liberal" media maintains a restrictive agenda. The goal is to program the mass consciousness, including the liberal establishment, who, like a herd of sheep, tend to believe whatever is

----

[7] "China and Viruses: The Case of Dr. Xiangguo Qiu; by Dany Shoham;" *Begin-Sadat Center for Strategic Studies* (2020)

[8] "The new coronavirus was not man-made, study shows: New research finds that SARS-CoV-2, the new coronavirus that causes COVID-19, is the result of the natural process of evolution rather than a product of laboratory engineering;" *Medical News Today* (2020)

presented to them in outlets like CNN, *The New York Times*, *Scientific American*, and *The New Yorker*.

As reported in DefenseOne[9], over the last years the People's Liberation Army, a.k.a the Chinese military, has made biological war and the development of bioweapons, which can be used to wage "asymmetric warfare," a central focus. As Elsa B Kania and Wilson Vordnick write in 'Weaponizing Biotech: How China's Military is Preparing for a 'New Domain of Warfare,' China's new strategy is to fuse military and civil activity, focusing on research in areas like gene editing, viral warfare, and neural implants:

"In 2010's War for Biological Dominance (制生权战争), Guo Jiwei (郭继卫), a professor with the Third Military Medical University, emphasizes the impact of biology on future warfare.

In 2015, then-president of the Academy of Military Medical Sciences He Fuchu (贺福初) argued that biotechnology will become the new "strategic commanding heights" of national defense, from biomaterials to "brain control" weapons. Maj. Gen. He has since become the vice president of the Academy of Military Sciences, which leads China's military science enterprise.

Biology is among seven "new domains of warfare" discussed in a 2017 book by Zhang Shibo (张仕波), a retired general and former president of the National Defense University, who concludes: "Modern biotechnology development is gradually showing

---

9 "Weaponizing Biotech: How China's Military Is Preparing for a 'New Domain of Warfare': Under Beijing's civil-military fusion strategy, the PLA is sponsoring research on gene editing, human performance enhancement, and more;" by Elsa B Kania and Wilson Vordnick; *DefenseOne* (2019)

strong signs characteristic of an offensive capability," including the possibility that "specific ethnic genetic attacks" (特定种族基因攻击) could be employed.

The 2017 edition of Science of Military Strategy (战略学), a textbook published by the PLA's National Defense University that is considered to be relatively authoritative, debuted a section about biology as a domain of military struggle, similarly mentioning the potential for new kinds of biological warfare to include "specific ethnic genetic attacks." "

The People's Liberation Army, in other words, has been working on "new kinds of biological warfare," such as lethal viruses, that target particular ethnic groups or demographics. While, once again, we don't know that Coronavirus-19 was intentionally released as a weapon of this sort, it is interesting to note that the fatality rate among certain communities, like those of African heritage, seems to be much higher than average. At the same time, the elderly and infirm — anyone already suffering from pre-existing conditions — are in much greater danger from this virus.

Whether or not the release of Coronavirus-19 was accidental or intentional (as at least one whistle-blowing Chinese virologist claims publically[10]), it seems well-documented that, once it was unleashed, President Xi Jiping and the Chinese military decided to let it travel around the world. According to *The Economic Times of India*, "There is new evidence to

---

[10] "Chinese virologist accuses Beijing of coronavirus cover-up, flees Hong Kong: 'I know how they treat whistleblowers': Li-Meng Yan told Fox News that she believes China knew about the coronavirus well before it claimed it did. She says her supervisors also ignored research she was doing that she believes could have saved lives;" by Barnini Chakraborty and Alex Diaz; *Fox News* (2020)

show that China locked down all domestic traffic internally by end January 2020 but pushed to open foreign travel till end March. Data from Tom Tom traffic index, a traffic location site that covers 416 cities across 57 countries show that as a result of this strategy, China, intentionally or otherwise, was able to lockdown its cities unknown to the world. While this reduced the spread of the Corona virus within China, China's aggressive foreign travel policy lead to a virus explosion worldwide."[11]

In the months after China stopped all domestic flights, Chinese Ambassadors in Italy, Australia[12], and elsewhere argued vehemently against international travel bans: "While Chinese authorities limited domestic flights from Wuhan to other Chinese cities like Beijing and Shanghai in an effort to contain the outbreak in January, it urged international carriers to maintain their flying schedules." Chinese Ambassadors threatened countries with reprisals if they banned flights from China.

I find the likeliest scenario to be that the initial release of Coronavirus-19 was accidental (apparently the safety protocols of the Wuhan Virology Institute were incredibly lax, perhaps intentionally so). Once it was released, the Chinese leadership decided to make use of the event as a real-time opportunity to discover what happens in such a circumstance: How would the international community respond, what

---

[11] "How China locked down internally for COVID-19, but pushed foreign travel;" by Sandip Sen; *The Times of India* (2020)

[12] "Chinese Ambassador to Australia Pleads for Easing of Coronavirus Travel Restrictions;" by Colin Packham; *Reuters*; February 17, 2020

level of damage would be created, and so on. They
are certainly learning a great deal about viral
contagion, fatality rates, societal impacts, and the
human immune response to engineered pathogens.

We might ask, how could human beings do such an
evil thing? The answer is obvious: The rulers of
China, as in many countries around the world today,
are psychopaths with no empathy for human
suffering at any scale. This already seems well-
established by China's actions in other areas, such as
its brutal suppression of ethnic minorities in Tibet
and elsewhere. And in fact, since the Chinese military
considers the United States as its most powerful
enemy, their strategy has proved amazingly effective,
causing economic and social turmoil in the US.

A compelling tangent in all of this is the peculiar
story of Charles Lieber, the former Chair of Harvard
University's Chemistry and Chemical Biology
Department and a leading nanotechnology expert.
Lieber was arrested in Massachusetts last winter for
setting up a secret laboratory in Wuhan. According to
CNBC[13], Lieber was receiving $50,000 a month from
the Chinese government and had established a
research lab at the Wuhan University of Technology
with a $1.5 million fund.

What is so peculiar about this is that Lieber was
extremely successful with his work in the US. His
research firm had received more than $15 million in
grants from the National Institutes of Health and
Department of Defense. He ran a Department at
Harvard. So why choose to operate secretly, and
illegally, in China?

---

[13] "Harvard professor indicted for allegedly making false
statements about secret work in Wuhan;" by Amanda Macias;
CNBC.com; June 9, 2020

It doesn't seem likely that Lieber was directly connected to the Wuhan Virology Institute or coronavirus research, as some theorists have proposed. He works in a different field, but one that has ominous relevance to the military goals of the People's Liberation Army, as described above. According to a 2018 interview with Lieber conducted by Nautilus Magazine[14], he is developing something called Neural Lace, "a lace-like electronic mesh that "you could literally inject" into three-dimensional synthetic and biological structures like the brain."

Lieber has already demonstrated that "mesh-brain implants readily integrate into a mouse brain and enable neuronal recordings for at least eight months." In a 2018 paper in Current Opinion in Neurobiology, Lieber co-authored a paper with several Chinese scientists titled Mesh Electronics: a new paradigm for tissue-like brain probes[15]. They write: "To bridge the gap between neural and electronic networks, we have introduced the new concept of mesh electronics probes designed with structural and mechanical properties such that the implant begins to 'look and behave' like neural tissue. Syringe-implanted mesh electronics have led to the realization of probes that are neuro-attractive and free of the chronic immune response, as well as capable of stable long-term mapping and modulation of brain activity at the single-neuron level."

---

[14] "Will This "Neural Lace" Brain Implant Help Us Compete with AI?;" by Kiki Sanford; *Nautilus*; August 29, 2016

[15] "Mesh electronics: a new paradigm for tissue-like brain probes;" by Guosong Hong, Xiao Yang, Tao Zhou and Charles M Lieber; *Current Opinion in Neurobiology* (2018)

While such probes could be potentially used to treat neurological disorders, they could also be used as tools to control a human being from within their own brain. Individuals would become drones, prosthetic instruments of a control apparatus. If you are the ruler of a totalitarian society like China and want to maintain control over a vast population, the possibility that "syringe-injectable electronics" can unfold into a three-dimensional neural mesh that controls your subjects' brains from inside has to be very intriguing to you.

I realize this sounds like dystopian science fiction or something from a horror film. Unfortunately, the reality is that this research is happening now, and it seems to be advancing rapidly. One problem is that we don't know how far it has advanced.

What is clear, in retrospect, is that the neoliberal approach to China, which we saw under Obama and Clinton, failed spectacularly. Obama and his predecessors pursued a policy of appeasement and conciliation with China, rather than challenging their growing power and influence in the world directly. This was clear in the negotiated Paris Accords, which gave China a long runway before it would need to limit CO2 production. America had become financially dependent on China and neoliberals did not feel they could oppose it.

Presumably the original hope with this policy was that Western liberal values — transmitted via technology, media, and consumerism — would eventually influence China and bring about its liberalization. In practice, however, this has not occurred. Under the autocratic rule of Xi Jinping, the Chinese government explicitly rejected core elements of the Western model such as the free press, the concept of universal human values, basic human rights, and an independent judiciary.

If anything, it appears that Western nation-states are tilting toward China, with increasing authoritarianism and surveillance, suppression of civil rights, and so on. A technological control apparatus seems, increasingly, inescapable. We are already there to some extent, as our Smart Phones and social networks function superbly as tracking and surveillance tools.

5. NEOLIBERAL TECHNOCRATS VERSUS LIBERTARIAN PLUTOCRATS

I consider it morally necessary, even in the face of so many drastic developments and sinister trends, to map out an alternative and better direction that human society could still take, as well as a plausible path for getting us there. This requires a unified popular movement as well as a cohesive initiative on the part of the progressive wealth-holding elite. I will do that toward the end of this essay. Before we can get there, let's delve into the background of the situation in the United States in a little more detail, among other topics.

There have been a few major "behind the scenes" influences on the direction of American society and its political economy over the last decades. The political spectrum in the US ranges from the Far Right to neoconservatism to neoliberalism to a few Left Wing outliers like Bernie Sanders and Alexandria Ocasio Cortez. Further to the Left are a small group of scraggly anarchists and a few left-over Marxists. The country has shifted ever-farther Right since 1980. Bill Clinton was essentially a "Republican Lite;" Obama as well.

One organization lurking behind the scenes is the
infamous Trilateral Commission, started by David
Rockefeller and Zbigniew Brzezinski in 1973 to build
cooperation between America, Western Europe, and
Japan. According to *The Washington Post*, its members
have included George W. Bush, Jimmy Carter, Al
Gore, Jeffrey Epstein, Paul Volcker, as well as "top
executives of AT&T, ITT, Xerox, Mobil, Exxon, the
Chase Manhattan Bank, First Chicago Corp., General
Electric, TRW, Archer Daniels Midland, PepsiCo, RJR
Nabisco and Goldman Sachs (not to mention Nissan,
Toshiba and Fuji Bank)."[16] The Trilateral Commission
published The Crisis of Democracy in 1975. The
report argued that Democratic society was becoming
unmanageable: "Some of the problems in the United
States today stem from an excess of democracy…"
the authors noted. "Needed, instead, is a greater
moderation in democracy." The Trilateral
Commission saw it in the best interests of the US,
European nations, and Japan to be directed by a
technocratic managerial elite, wielding power outside
of the turbulence of electoral politics.

The Trilateral Commission is often made a central
focus of conspiracy theories. That is not my interest
here. The point I want to make is that one important
strain in American political thought has been shaped
by a particular contingent within the power elite. This
influential group believe that our future direction is
not toward more democracy, but less. We will
inevitably become a technological society, a
technocracy, managed for the masses by a small group

---

16 "BEWARE THE TRILATERAL COMMISSION!;" by David
Mills: *Washington Post* (April 25, 1992)

of elite experts that includes corporate executives and the super-wealthy, with elections largely irrelevant.

Whether or not the Trilateral Commission is still as powerful, this type of technocratic approach is pursued today by the neoliberal elite in the Democratic party, as well as sectors of Wall Street and Silicon Valley. People like Eric Schmidt of Google and Bill Gates align with this technocratic, managerial agenda and worldview. We are seeing growing fury against this technocratic approach from the mass populace, who see it as distanced, arrogant, and against their interests. Working people, for instance, are afraid of increasing automation, such as self-driving cars and trucks, which will take away their jobs. Their fury is being manipulated and channeled into irrational conspiracy theories like Qanon, which has become a large-scale problem, and also erupting in new social movements like the The Gilets Jaunes or Yellow Jackets in France.

Another extremely powerful cabal is made up of wealthy Far Right Libertarians. The enormous influence wielded by this group was the subject of Jane Mayer's indispensable book, Dark Money. Essentially, in the 1960s, a group of super wealthy businessmen, led by the Koch brothers, realized they did not like the direction of American society. They hated the Great Society program with its increases in social services, increased taxation on the wealthy, better public health and public education. They met in secret and developed a strategic and tactical plan, orchestrated like a corporate takeover, to strip away these programs. As explicitly laid out in the Powell Memorandum, they wanted to radically limit the power of government.

To this end, they funded economics departments at universities and think tanks like the Heritage Foundation, built lobbying arms and media outlets. They realized they needed Conservative initiatives that resembled the grassroots activist movements found on the Left, so they created "astro-turf'd" social movements like the Tea Party. They strategically backed certain intellectuals like Charles Murray, author of The Bell Curve, which correlates IQ to race. Murray's work has been repeatedly debunked. But it provides ideological cover for reducing social services and educations to certain ethnic groups, such as blacks.

While the Libertarian plutocrats did not entirely support Trump at first, they aligned with him after his election. Many of Trump's cabinet appointees have close ties to the Heritage Foundation. Trump's cabinet are mainly tasked with reducing their departments to the bare minimum, if not eliminating their function altogether. The Koch brothers' forty-plus year strategy finally succeeded. Trump unified the Republican Party around a neo-Fascist agenda and personality cult, seeking to establish rule by a minority over the long term.

Both the technocratic neoliberal approach represented by Obama, the Clintons, and Biden and the Right Wing libertarian approach represented by Trump have revealed themselves to be catastrophic failures for the United States and the world. Both seek a controlled or managed pseudo-Democracy, rather than a system that empowers the people and limits the influence of wealthy elites. Obama, with a large-scale popular mandate and a Democratic majority in Congress, was unable to address the ecological emergency we are facing, which threatens humanity

with civilizational collapse and extinction, or reduce
wealth inequality. In his Nobel Peace Prize speech, he
argued for "just wars." Since leaving office, Obama
has bragged that he counts fracking, which causes
irreparable environmental harm, and increasing Wall
Street's dividends among his successes. It was the
Neoliberal's sell-out of the working class that paved
the way for Trumpism.

6. CONSPIRANOIA

Many of us have been watching, with increasing apprehension, the viral spread of convoluted conspiracy theories such as Qanon, Pizzagate, and "Plandemic." The proliferation of these theories reflects a dangerous collapse of coherence. However, there is also something positive about this phenomenon. We are seeing a growing revulsion against the direction of post-industrial society. Increasingly, people from across the political spectrum feel an intense, instinctual aversion to the forward march of corporate globalization and technocratic neoliberalism. They are desperately seeking a meaningful alternative, an answer. This, in itself, is a good thing.

People know that our society has gone off the rails, even if they don't have the tools to fully understand how and why. They realize corruption is endemic within our financial system and governing bodies, while the mass media spreads calculated deceptions. When people feel angry, frustrated, and betrayed, they gravitate to conspiracy theories, such as Qanon and Pizzagate, which give them a focus for their anger and propose a counter-mythology. Unfortunately, these narratives, while containing kernels of truth, have been weaponized by interests aligned with the Far Right, probably Russian agents as well.

People have been hooked by AI-powered algorithms designed to target their psychological biases and weak points. Conspiracy narratives are being used as weapons to drive us further toward social breakdown, violence, and authoritarian rule. If people can understand how and why they are being manipulated, they may be able to shift their rage onto the right targets.

According to Qanon, the neoliberal elite in government, Hollywood, and Silicon Valley include active Satanists, fixated on the sexual abuse of children, performing ritual abuse and cannibalism. This seems outlandish to those who maintain any faith in the establishment narrative, which Jordan Hall calls the "Blue Church." The problem is that the Jeffrey Epstein scandal — as well as the horrific Jimmy Saville scandal in Britain, which preceded it — reveals an undeniable kernel of truth to some of this. Hollywood has also had pedophilia scandals.

It can't be purely an accident that Epstein was so closely linked to the Clintons, Bill Gates, Trump, Dershowitz, Prince Andrew, as well as institutions like Harvard and MIT — the list goes on. It doesn't matter whether all of Epstein's friends actively participated in pedophilia, although it seems clear that some — notably Trump, Dershowitz and Prince Andrew — did participate. All of these individuals share at least the tacit agreement that those with money and power can act with impunity, disregarding laws and social norms. Apparently, none of them cared to inquire into how Epstein made his fortune. A tacit belief shared by all of them is, "The ends justify the means."

It seems reasonable to conclude that something else is going on, under the surface and perhaps outside of conscious intent. As someone whose perspective is informed by shamanism and the occult, I might propose that, at another level of consciousness, an occult bond connects those who control and manipulate the masses. Epstein's bizarre temple on "pedo island," suggests, whether he knew it consciously or not, that his illicit activities with the power elite held an esoteric significance. As well as assembling "Kompromat" for Mossad, Epstein and his friends were subliminally aligning with dark powers.

It is conceivable that a form of malevolent occultism, requiring rituals of abuse and forms of sacrifice, underlies our political control system. Many have wondered about secretive institutions like Skull and Bones and Bohemian Grove. The elite congregate in these places to engage in ceremonies. The participants themselves may not realize that the true function of these hazing rituals is to make contact with occult intelligences. Such events tend to take place in a lowered state of consciousness, fueled by alcohol. In this lowered state of consciousness, bonds can be created with entities and regressive occult forces who seek control over the human herd for their own purposes.

I realize, from within the mainstream neoliberal ideology of scientific materialism, such a prospect seems impossible and even silly. But this is why so many people are getting frustrated and enraged, abandoning "rationalism" and signing on to conspiracy theories: They feel a huge gap between their basic intuition about what is happening and the mainstream or establishment worldview, which refuses to make sense of it. This schism opens the gateway for Fascism, which at least speaks to the unconscious and acknowledges hidden or occult layers of reality. Trump does this quite effectively and melodramatically (as when he said there were dark shadowy forces supporting Biden from behind the scenes). Constricted by their scientific materialist ideology, establishment liberals are unable to respond authentically to the hidden or occult dimensions of what is taking place — the archetypal forces being summoned and unleashed into the collective Psyche.

There are huge holes in the various conspiracy theories, but their growing popularity reveals a deeper shift. We are starting to see a mass revulsion against the direction of technocracy. People feel betrayed. Their intuition tells them something is deeply wrong, even if they cannot identify what it is. They want to tear down and destroy the existing structures, to purge and cleanse and start anew. Without an accurate assessment of what is happening or a working model of an alternative, this will only cause more destruction.

Unfortunately, Qanon believers are being manipulated by those who wish to establish an even more oppressive system of control. Indeed, the current collapse of coherence is reminiscent of Europe in the 1930s. Nazi-ism also developed out of a murky occult ideology mingled with conspiracy theories, absorbed from the Thule Society, Theosophy, and elsewhere. The '30s Fascist movement was also driven by the frustration of the masses, who felt their hopes for the future had been betrayed. These regressive movements tend to culminate in collective "ceremonies" of mass violence, such as civil wars and genocides. This is a kind of ritualized expression we should try to avoid if possible, particularly in a world bristling with nuclear and biological weapons.

To reach a different outcome, we have to define a new, creative approach to our situation and build a movement around it. We need to map out a new ideological position, develop alliances, and then shape communicative techniques and strategies around a unifying agenda and goal. An authentic counter-movement must promote an inspiring alternative that doesn't reject, but acknowledges and integrates, the dark matter of the unconscious and the occult, as Qanon does, while leading humanity back onto an evolutionary path toward peace, social justice, ecological regeneration, and reduced inequality.

This requires addressing the corruption, hypocrisy, and flawed ideology on the part of neoliberals, technocrats, and the Right Wing. We must assimilate what is meaningful in the current spate of virulent conspiracy theories, and reject much that is fantasy. We also need to challenge the prevailing orthodoxies of Capitalism and "progress," along with areas such as technology development and public health, from a perspective guided by logic and reason, informed by empathy and compassion. The goal is to unify many factions who do not perceive their shared interests as of yet, around a singular mission and strategic agenda.

I know that this seems daunting; hard to imagine and extremely difficult to achieve. However if we can conceive of it, perhaps we can manifest it. Crisis allows for previously impossible ideas to be embraced and realized. The alternative is dire: An unstoppable slide into incoherence, collective violence, and Fascism as our ecological systems break down around us. We are entering a time when we need global unity and a sense of shared purpose like never before.

49

7. IS BILL GATES THE DEVIL?

Popular conspiracy theories demonize Bill Gates. According to this view, which the alternative news site The Corbett Report defined in a series of videos, Gates is an evil mastermind. He is the successor of David Rockefeller, another empire builder who used philanthropy to advance his global control agenda. Conspiracists believe that Gates actively plans to depopulate Africa and other parts of the developing world. They see his end game as totalitarian control of the global population through vaccines and biometric chips that will control our access to money, allowing us to travel or trade. China has already implemented elements of such a system, with their social credit scores.

The conspiracy theories offer an exaggerated caricature of Gates' position. The Corbett Report videos make some interesting points but, on close inspection, they are riddled with false information. At the same time, there are legitimate reasons to be worried about Gates' agenda and to question his extraordinary power and influence. The work of the

Gates Foundation needs to be critically analyzed and carefully parsed.

Gates has become the world's leading exemplar of "philanthro-capitalism," the seamless melding of commercial interests with charitable ones. Interestingly, as Gates has given away billions of dollars of his wealth, gaining extraordinary social prestige in the process, his net worth has greatly increased. Through the Gates Foundation over the last decades, he and his wife Melinda have promulgated their belief that the world is steadily improving, arguing that poverty is retreating across the planet. "By almost any measure, the world is better than it has ever been," Gates wrote in his 2014 Gates Annual Letter. "People are living longer, healthier lives. Many nations that were aid recipients are now self-sufficient… Many—though by no means all—of the countries we used to call poor now have thriving economies. And the percentage of very poor people has dropped by more than half since 1990."

Their analysis is questionable. In The Guardian[17], economist Jason Hickel argues that the statistics favored by Bill Gates, Karl Schwab, Steven Pinker, and other members of the global elite who congregate at the World Economic Forum in Davos each year, must be interpreted differently. For instance, according to one graph, "the proportion of people living in poverty has declined from 94% in 1820 to only 10% today." Gates and his cronies use such statistics to make the case that "we shouldn't complain about rising inequality when the very forces that deliver such immense wealth to the richest are

---

[17] "Bill Gates says poverty is decreasing. He couldn't be more wrong;" by Jason Hickel; *The Guardian* (2019)

also eradicating poverty before our very eyes." For Hickel, the numbers actually reveal that "the world went from a situation where most of humanity had no need of money at all to one where today most of humanity struggles to survive on extremely small amounts of money." There was no decline in poverty. Instead, "there was a process of dispossession that bulldozed people into the capitalist labour system, during the enclosure movements in Europe and the colonisation of the global south."

The view of linear progress favored by Gates and the WEF also fails to include Capitalism's catastrophic ecological impacts, which are increasingly evident. In essence, the world traded a veneer of short-term prosperity for inevitable long-term collapse. Hunger, infectious disease, and poverty were never close to being eliminated. They are now roaring back.

Over the last half-century, post-industrial civilization became fixated on unleashing the power of technology at the expense of developing a truly holistic, ethical framework that would make it possible for humans to live in peaceful solidarity. The success of Silicon Valley — IBM, Microsoft, Apple, Google, Facebook, Amazon, and so on — fueled the fantasy that technology, divorced from any moral vision or purpose, was, in itself, a positive force. This ideology was laid out in *Wired Magazine* and in books like Kevin Kelly's *What Technology Wants*, Peter Diamandis' *Abundance*, and Ray Kurzweil's *The Singularity Is Near*.

We were told that all we had to do was leave the engineers and venture capitalists alone, and they would lead humanity to a fabulous techno-utopia beyond our wildest dreams. The Singularity — that approaching "omega point" where humans merge

with machines or get replaced by machine sentience
— became the religious faith of Silicon Valley.
Despite all of the evidence that what we are
accelerating heedlessly toward is not even an artificial
paradise — more like a mechanized hell-scape — this
ideology remains firmly in place among the
Libertarian tech elite.

I do not think that Gates is a super villain who
intentionally plots to use enforced vaccinations and
bio-chips as an instrument of absolute global
domination and depopulation. He is better
understood as a hyper-rational atheist who believes in
science, technology, and Capitalism as forces for
linear, exponential progress. He approaches the world
through the limited lens defined by his own wealth
and success as a corporate overlord. He sees himself
(as the recent Netflix documentary series about him,
which he authorized, seeks to make him out) as a kind
of heroic nerd, determined to use his much-vaunted
brain to solve humanity's biggest challenges. He wants
to carve out a place for himself in history and
perhaps become the richest man in history. This is the
competitive game he seeks to win. His philanthropic
"generosity" is tainted by his unaddressed shadow: A
tyrannical quest for control, an arrogant conviction in
his superior ability, an enormous ego, and an inability
to question the fundamental structure of Capitalism
itself.

We know that the level at which we operate as
conscious beings is just one level: Consciousness, as
Carl Jung explored, is only a small circle of light
within the dark ocean of the unconscious mind. Men
like Gates and Zuckerberg amassed gigantic fortunes
because they were allowed to privatize aspects of the
commons. The Internet was built by public funds, by

taxpayers. Its founders, such as Tim Berners-Lee, intended it to be an open architecture supporting collaboration and progress. While it has allowed for some of that, the Internet also became an extraordinary tool for private wealth creation. Instead of developing in an open source way, the Internet today is confined by endless pay walls, patented software, and exclusive silos. Gates has benefited tremendously from this act of public largesse.

In his philanthropy, Gates seeks to impose the hyper-masculine, rational, binary engineering logic that made him fantastically wealthy onto the world's biggest problems. This inevitably creates a slew of negative results. In Bill Gates' Charity Paradox[18], an investigation into Gates' "$50 billion charitable enterprise," *The Nation*'s Tim Schwab found that "Gates's outsize charitable giving — $36 billion to date — has created a blinding halo effect around his philanthropic work, as many of the institutions best placed to scrutinize his foundation are now funded by Gates, including academic think tanks that churn out uncritical reviews of its charitable efforts and news outlets that praise its giving or pass on investigating its influence. In the absence of outside scrutiny, this private foundation has had far-reaching effects on public policy, pushing privately run charter schools into states where courts and voters have rejected them, using earmarked funds to direct the World Health Organization to work on the foundation's global health agenda, and subsidizing Merck's and Bayer's entry into developing countries."

---

[18] "Bill Gates's Charity Paradox: *A Nation* investigation illustrates the moral hazards surrounding the Gates Foundation's $50 billion charitable enterprise;" by Tim Schwab; *The Nation;* March 17, 2020

The Gates Foundation has given around $250 million in charitable grants to companies in which the foundation holds corporate stocks and bonds. These include pharmaceutical companies such as Merck, Novartis, and GlaxoSmithKline, along with many other corporations. The grants are directed "at projects like developing new drugs and health monitoring systems and creating mobile banking services." Many of these initiatives have the potential to provide ancillary financial benefit to Gates himself. Gates has also invested over $250 million into media such as NPR and Participant Films (who produced the Netflix documentary series on him), buying himself a great deal of influence over coverage of his activities. Gates has gained inordinate influence over public policy through his donations, such as his support of the World Health Organization.

Writing in *The Nation*, journalist Charles Pillar exposed the "puzzling ethical blind spot" in the management of the Gates Foundation's $40 billion endowment: The Foundation "reaped vast profits by placing billions of dollars in firms whose activities and products subverted the foundation's good works." [19] The contradictions, as Pillar lays them out, are excruciatingly glaring:

"Gates donated $218 million to prevent polio and measles in places like the Niger Delta, yet invested $423 million in the oil companies whose delta pollution literally kills the children the foundation tries to help. It had vast holdings in Big Pharma firms that priced AIDS drugs out of reach for desperate

---

[19] "How the Gates Foundation's Investments Are Undermining Its Own Good Works: Its vast holdings in the fossil fuel and arms industries subvert the foundation's battle against disease and poverty;" by Charles Pillar; *The Nation*; August 22, 2014

victims the foundation wanted to save. It benefited greatly from predatory lenders whose practices sparked the Great Recession and chocolate makers said by the US government to have supported child slavery in Ivory Coast. ... The Gates Foundation boasts about its grants to help poor farmers adapt to droughts and floods caused by global warming. Yet according to the foundation's most recent tax filing and recent SEC filings, it holds more than $1.2 billion in a rogues' gallery of corporate actors, including BP, Royal Dutch Shell and Exxon Mobil, whose environmental despoliation promotes the climate change that is destroying those farmers' livelihoods."

Either Gates retains total faith in the model of corporate Capitalism as a force for good in the world, which makes him blind to these glaring contradictions, or he does have a darker and more hidden agenda, as conspiracy theorists propose. In interviews, he brags about the enormous financial return on investment that his Foundation receives from vaccines. Gates and his wife have built a public health empire where they hold tremendous power and influence over policy, drug development, and in other areas, yet they are not experts in the field nor have they been chosen by the people, through an open democratic process, to serve in this role.

Conspiracy theorists who argue that Gates has a depopulation agenda often focus on one comment he made in a TED talk, where he said better public health could reduce over-population in the developing world. This comment has been taken out of context. His point comes from evolutionary psychology: When women know their children are more likely to survive into adulthood, they don't have as many children, which naturally reduces the birthrate. I find this a reasonable perspective and not a reason to pillory him. What seems deeply problematic, however, is the ambiguous relationship between Gates' hyper-Capitalism and his philanthropy, as well as his imposition of a binary engineering logic onto complex social problems, which inevitably creates new, worse problems (as so much of technology does). Our current model, which puts great power and influence over public policy into the hands of those who have amassed wealth through private enterprise (in Gates' case, through cut-throat monopolistic practices and protection of patents), is neither workable nor sustainable.

This brings us to the hot-button subject of vaccines. Personally, I believe that vaccines, like those against Polio and Smallpox, were major achievements of modern medicine, eradicating terrible scourges. The problem is that, since the mid-1980s, the number of vaccines that children receive has skyrocketed. Children used to get seven shots. Now they receive more than 70, treating at least 16 diseases. The profits that pharmaceutical companies make from vaccines has also skyrocketed. Vaccines now generate $60 billion per year in revenue.

In that same period, from the mid-1980s until today, the health of children in the US has not improved but has in fact worsened. Extreme autism is one of the most horrible conditions that has skyrocketed in the last decades. In some areas of the US, one in 54 children and at least one in 22 boys now develop autism, compared to perhaps one in a thousand or less, back in the 1970s. On the edge of the spectrum, Autism is a debilitating condition that utterly ruins people's lives. Parents have to care for a mentally incapacitated child who becomes an adult unable to control their emotions or, in many cases, even their bodily functions. In the US, autism rates are progressing so fast that we are a few decades away from one out of two children having this condition, if current trends persist.

According to mainstream medicine, there is no known correlation between the proliferation of vaccines and autism as well as other chronic conditions that our children are now developing in vast numbers, such as asthma and ADHD. Yet the known "adverse events" and possible side effects for the Tripedia vaccine, which covers diphtheria, tetanus and pertussis, include "SIDS, anaphylactic reaction cellulitis, autism, convulsion/grand mal convulsion, encephalopathy, hypotonia, neuropathy, somnolence and apnea." According to the website RXList.com: "Because these events are reported voluntarily from a population of uncertain size, it is not always possible to reliably estimate their frequencies or to establish a causal relationship."

People have good reason not to trust pharmaceutical companies. Capitalism evolved into a far more predatory form over the last decades. Today, publicly traded companies are locked into a short-term, profit-seeking agenda and must keep inflating the value of their stocks. The inescapable logic of the financial system forces corporations to behave like diabolical predators. Due to their fiduciary responsibility, companies must maximize shareholder value at all costs, even if this means ignoring all externalities, such as health, safety, and long-term ecological consequences.

Publicly traded corporations that manufacture cigarettes, like Phillip Morris, knew for many decades that their product killed their customers in large numbers. They hid the data and fought lawsuits to protect their profits. Similarly, the executives of fossil fuel companies, like British Petroleum and Occidental, are well aware that accelerating climate change caused by CO2 emissions will make most of the planet unlivable within a few decades. Facebook and Twitter know that the addictive dopamine hits caused by fake news are horrible for society but boost their advertising revenue. And these are just a few of the negative "externalities" we are aware of.

Considering this, why is it impossible for the liberal establishment to consider whether or not the major pharmaceutical companies who manufacture vaccines have a shady agenda? They have poor track records in other areas. For example, Merck is one of the main pharmaceutical companies manufacturing vaccines. Twenty years ago, Merck mass-distributed Vioxx, a headache drug. Vioxx caused up to 500,000 US deaths from heart attacks, as an article from The Week[20] documents. As Robert F Kennedy Jr notes and the article substantiates, Merck was well aware that Vioxx was going to kill a lot of people. They continued to distribute the drug because they assessed it would make them more profit than they would lose in eventual lawsuits. Merck is one of the main US companies benefiting from the $60 billion annual windfall from vaccines.

When we realize that the pharmaceutical companies we entrust with our children's health are willing to commit mass murder for profit, we must consider the recent proliferation of vaccines in a different light.

---

[20] "When half a million Americans died and nobody noticed: Was the US drug Vioxx responsible for far more deaths than has been acknowledged so far?;" by Alexander Cockburn; *The Week*; April 27, 2012

What if top executives at these corporations are well aware of the potential dangers of new vaccines, yet have calculated the profit and loss and found it benefits their bottom line? What if they simply don't care to investigate, as they know that skyrocketing rates of chronic conditions like Autism, asthma, and ADHD, if they occur, will benefit them?

As Kennedy points out, the same companies that make vaccines also manufacture drugs used to treat chronic conditions. A lifelong sufferer of asthma, ADHD, or autism may lead a miserable life, but they provide a constant profit stream for drug companies. The epidemic in synthetic opioid addiction, devastating for so many families and communities, increases profits for drug companies.

Kennedy, director of the Children's Defense Fund, is a complex figure. He has become the leading public figure speaking out against Bill Gates, the pharmaceutical industry, and the increased use of vaccinations. He also believes that the international response to the Coronavirus pandemic has been an intentional over-reaction designed to disempower the populace and bring about a greater level of social control. He receives constant criticism from the mainstream media and medical establishment, as well as occasional censorship or "shadow banning" for some of his proclamations. While some of his assertions, such as his statements about Vioxx, check out as accurate, others seem to be exaggerated. However well-founded their concerns, a certain degree of hysteria seems to be the case with many in the "Anti-Vaxx" / 5G conspiracy camp, which muddies their argument and reduces the effectiveness of their critiques.

Kennedy posted a long post about Gates on Instagram, his principle tool for public communication: "Vaccines, for Bill Gates, are a strategic philanthropy that feed his many vaccine-related businesses (including Microsoft's ambition to control a global vac ID enterprise) and give him dictatorial control over global health policy — the spear tip of corporate neo-imperialism. Gates' obsession with vaccines seems fueled by a messianic conviction that he is ordained to save the world with technology and a god-like willingness to experiment with the lives of lesser humans." Kennedy goes on to list a series of public health crises in the developing world that he claims were caused by Gates-funded vaccines.[21]

It is difficult to ascertain whether all of Kennedy's claims are accurate. And even if they are accurate, he

---

[21] According to Kennedy's Instagram post:

"Promising to eradicate Polio with $1.2 billion, Gates took control of India's National Advisory Board (NAB) and mandated 50 polio vaccines (up from 5) to every child before age 5. Indian doctors blame the Gates campaign for a devastating vaccine-strain polio epidemic that paralyzed 496,000 children between 2000 and 2017.

In 2017, the Indian Government dialed back Gates' vaccine regimen and evicted Gates and his cronies from the NAB. Polio paralysis rates dropped precipitously.

In 2017, the World Health Organization reluctantly admitted that the global polio explosion is predominantly vaccine strain, meaning it is coming from Gates' Vaccine Program.

The most frightening epidemics in Congo, the Philippines, and Afghanistan are all linked to Gates' vaccines. By 2018, ¾ of global polio cases were from Gates' vaccines.

In 2014, the Gates Foundation funded tests of experimental HPV vaccines, developed by GSK and Merck, on 23,000 young girls in remote Indian provinces. Approximately 1,200 suffered severe side effects, including autoimmune and fertility disorders. Seven died.
Indian government investigations charged that Gates funded researchers committed pervasive ethical violations: pressuring vulnerable village girls into the trial, bullying parents, forging consent forms, and refusing medical care to the injured girls. The case is now in the country's Supreme Court.

In 2010, the Gates Foundation funded a trial of a GSK's experimental malaria vaccine, killing 151 African infants and causing serious adverse effects including paralysis, seizure, and febrile convulsions to 1,048 of the 5,049 children..."

seems to intentionally obscure any larger context. It is well known that vaccines carry some risks. A small proportion of those who receive them will develop diseases and negative side effects. It can be argued that vaccines still have a larger cumulative benefit to human health, even though they sometimes cause suffering and even death.

Kennedy writes. "In 2014, Kenya's Catholic Doctors Association accused the WHO of chemically sterilizing millions of unwilling Kenyan women with a phony "tetanus" vaccine campaign." There don't seem to be follow up newspaper articles or research papers substantiating this serious accusation. It would be much easier to support the value of Kennedy's arguments if he limited himself to carefully vetted source material. Instead he seems to be feeding fear and hysteria in some of his pronouncements.

And yet, at the same time, his analysis has more merit than his detractors will allow. He writes: "Global public health advocates around the world accuse Gates of hijacking WHO's agenda away from the projects that are proven to curb infectious diseases; clean water, hygiene, nutrition and economic development.They say he has diverted agency resources to serve his personal fetish - that good health only comes in a syringe. In addition to using his philanthropy to control WHO, UNICEF, GAVI and PATH, Gates funds private pharmaceutical companies that manufacture vaccines, and a massive network of pharmaceutical-industry front groups that broadcast deceptive propaganda, develop fraudulent studies, conduct surveillance and psychological operations against vaccine hesitancy and use Gates' power and money to silence dissent and coerce compliance."

Gates is the major funder of Public Citizen, which, pre-Covid, put on a massive concert every year in Central Park, amassing resources toward its stated goal of ending poverty. However, unsurprisingly, Public Citizen doesn't address the issue of wealth inequality as a factor in poverty around the world.

According to conspiracy theories, Gates is developing implanted bio-sensors as well as biometric ID systems. While Gates has denied the claim that he supports a universal ID to be implanted under the skin, he definitely has an interest in biometric IDs as well as biological sensors that can be used for continuous monitoring of biological and emotional processes. The Gates Foundation touts biometric identification as a means to "enable more efficient and equitable resource distribution in developing nations." They have funded Veridium, a company which seeks to "design a new banking model, using our biometric authentication technology to bring the unbanked into the financial services system." While the agenda sounds superficially humanitarian, the tendency is toward greater monitoring and data collection, which leads inexorably toward more invasive social control.

Gates also funds the educational standards called Common Core, which many educators and parents find restrictive. As *The Washington Post* reported in 2014, "The Bill and Melinda Gates Foundation didn't just bankroll the development of what became known as the Common Core State Standards. With more than $200 million, the foundation also built political support across the country, persuading state governments to make systemic and costly changes." Common Core is a system of learning that promotes very limited, rote responses on standardized tests. It indoctrinates children, from an early age, into a reductive worldview, forcing them to regurgitate the exact words from written texts. As one critic notes[22], Common Core "suppresses freedom and boxes children into a systematic way of thinking."

Many agree that Common Core is a wrong direction for education. Focused on normative standards, it also programs children with the logic of transactional economics, indoctrinating them into the limited logic of Capitalist exchange. As part of the Common Core initiative, The Gates Foundation funded an electronic sensing bracelet that would monitor children's emotional responses, whether they remained interested or got bored during class. Like many Gates Foundation initiatives, the project seems excessively invasive and condescendingly patriarchal.

Gates may have interest in implantable bio-sensors for more general use. According to an extensive article in TAP Newswire[23], which is admittedly not the most reliable source, the Gates Foundation and the Department of Defense are developing "Implantable multi-analyte sensors for the continuous monitoring of body chemistries." (The article claims this language is taken directly from a Gates Foundation grant approval. However, I have been unable to confirm this.) Such implants, if mandated, would give governments an unprecedented level of control over their subjects. Our temperature and the

---

22 "Democracy & Education: A Democratic Critique of the Common Core English Language (ELA) Standards;" by Nicholas Tampio; *Democracy Education Journal* (2018)

23 "FDA Nears Approval of Injectable Biochip Implants for COVID Detection, Linked to Computers;" *TAP Newswire*; August, 2020

functioning of our organs would be constantly monitored, with that information transmitted to governing bodies.

In a society dominated by Capitalist exploitation, which concentrates wealth in the hands of the few, the super-wealthy operate according to their own agendas, without public oversight, civil society involvement, or democratic accountability. The self-contradictions of Capitalism have reached a point of absurdity, yet we lack for authentic public debates about other options for our future. In the United States, an intensive effort has demonized the concept of socialism, while ignoring the "corporate socialism" that gives huge handouts to corporations and financial institutions while ignoring the needs of the people.

8. BIOSECURITY IN A POST-POLITICAL WORLD

What people sense in Gates' technocratic approach in areas like health, education, and social welfare is the intensification of an ever-more invasive social control apparatus. We are seeing this agenda advance as a result of the Coronavirus pandemic in ways that seem intolerable, antithetical to our basic freedoms, for many Westerners. The Italian political philosopher Giorgio Agamben believes the global mobilization around the Coronavirus pandemic reveals a new political agenda which he calls biosecurity. The transition toward biosecurity, as a means of instituting totalitarian surveillance and population control, has been underway for quite a long time. As a post-political paradigm, it restricts the movement of bodies, goods, and information while governments gain unprecedented power over their subjects.

"It is evident that, apart from the emergency situation, linked to a certain virus that may in the future be replaced by another, at issue is the design of a paradigm of governance whose efficacy will exceed that of all forms of government known thus far in the political history of the West," Agamben writes. "If already, in the progressive decline of ideologies and political beliefs, security reasons allowed citizens to accept limitations on their liberty that they previously were unwilling to accept, biosecurity has shown itself capable of presenting the absolute cessation of all political activity and all social relations as the maximum form of civic participation."

Agamben notes that the pandemic panic led to "organizations of the left, traditionally in the habit of claiming rights and denouncing violations of the constitution, accepting limitations on liberty made by ministerial decree devoid of any legal basis and which even fascism couldn't dream of imposing." Why the Left has capitulated so immediately to the biosecurity agenda requires some unpacking.

In previous works, Agamben explored how we still linger under the shadow of the Holocaust and the nuclear bomb. Sovereign power is now defined by "bio-power": direct control over life and death. With the global response to the pandemic, we have indeed entered a new bio-political world, whose future remains to be seen. Unfortunately, it tends toward a nightmare of surveillance and control beyond anything Orwell ever dreamed.

Neoliberal technocrats, like most of those on the Left, are scientific materialists. From this perspective, protecting the individual's right to life — prolonging their "bare life" — is the only absolute value. This is reflected in the way our medical system seeks to extend the life of the elderly as long as possible, no matter the level of senescence or misery experienced by the individual. The institutional gravity of our medical system, with its capacity to extend life, remains an article of unquestionable faith for the neoliberal technocracy. This is why Blue Church believers stridently reject any possibility that vaccines could be causing harm. The occultist Rene Guenon named one of his books, *The Reign of Quantity*. A natural outcome of the scientific materialist worldview is a monomaniacal focus on quantified results like life extension, ignoring the quality or meaning of lived experience.

The developing biosecurity complex is a logical extension of the neoliberal technocratic worldview, which emerged from Capitalism and bourgeois society, fixated on creature comforts, convenience, and security. This culture sought to escape the omnipresent anxiety induced by materialist nihilism by hiding all signs of death, decay, and the void. All that mattered, in the end, was the privileged individual's immediate safety and security. In practice, this gave rise to the middle-class "nanny state" mandating everything from guardrails and safety helmets for children, to seatbelts and smoking bans for adults.

At least until the rise of Trumpism, the safety and security of the American citizen was given special privilege and status as part of the ideology of American exceptionalism. We saw this in the collective cultural response to 9–11 in the United States: We lavishly mourned 3,000 dead Americans, but entirely ignored one million Iraqi civilians who died as a result of our unjust and unnecessary war. The United States remains a caste society where certain human groups are accorded a much higher status — their privileges, their health and security seen as precious — while other human beings are treated as subhuman and do not matter at all. With Trumpism, the lower classes within the US are now treated in the same brusque way as we previously treated the people of Iraq, Afghanistan, Korea, Chile, Honduras, and so on: They are reduced to economic integers, subhumans, whose lives have minimal value. The privileged few, on the other hand, live beyond the law.

As it evolved, Neoliberal technocracy sought to remove the rough edges from life and the world, leaving something as vacuous as an endless Seinfeld episode. George Orwell thought that " a desirable civilization" would "aim at making life simpler and harder instead of softer and more complex." Our civilization — the one collapsing around us now — has done the opposite. It has left most of us brutally unprepared for the harsh conditions that will become the norm in the near future, as ecosystems break down and basic issues like access to food and fresh water become life or death questions, even in the developed world. The likely near-term scenario is covered in depth by Jim Bendell in his invaluable paper, Deep Adaptation: A Map for Navigating Climate Tragedy.

The Coronavirus pandemic is an extremely complex topic which continues to have many unknowns. The pandemic revealed the United States to be a partly failed state, compared to more regimented, homogenous, and well-organized societies like those in Western Europe and Asia, which took protection of their citizens seriously. Like those countries, the US should have instituted an immediate nationwide lockdown period to bring down transmission rates, followed by mask-wearing in supermarkets and public transport, with ongoing quarantine for those in the highest risk categories, but not for everyone.

America's failed response to the Coronavirus
revealed devastating flaws in a system excessively
focused on protecting private wealth and driving
capital accumulation. The failure of the United States
to manufacture and distribute basic health gear was
not due to a real-world lack of capacity. Our hyper-
capitalist system was unable to redirect privatized
resources efficiently toward sane, humane objectives.
The pandemic revealed the American system as
morally bankrupt and excessively unjust. Of course,
this was already evident. The pandemic just made it
more glaringly obvious.

At the same time, we should at least consider
Agamben and Kennedy's argument that the global
response to the pandemic is a quasi-intentional over-
reaction, establishing a new level of social control, a
post-political regime based on biosecurity. More and
more data seems to reveal that Covid-19, while highly
communicable, is, for younger demographics, only
slightly more dangerous than the flu. On September
2, 2020, CNN reported that, by the CDC's "current
best estimate about viral transmission and disease
severity in the United States"… "0.4% of people who
feel sick with Covid-19 will die. For people age 65 and
older, the CDC puts that number at 1.3%. For people
49 and under, the agency estimated that 0.05% of
symptomatic people will die."[24] The concern that
survivors of Covid often experience long-term
damage to organs also seems over-hyped. The same is
also true for the flu in a similarly small number of
cases. In "Data Quality Issues and the Coronavirus
Pandemic," an article on Medium, Tam Hunt, a

---

[24] "CDC estimates that 35% of coronavirus patients don't
have symptoms;" by Arman Azad, *CNN*; May 22, 2020

scientist and independent researcher, analyzes the data and concludes that US institutions are "significantly over-stating (not under-stating) the severity of the pandemic." Obviously this is an extremely complex topic, as little was known about the virus at first.

As Kennedy rightly notes, the tragic reality is that the response to Coronavirus is destined to have far more fatal and destructive consequences than the virus itself. A recent article from CNBC titled, U.N. warns of 'hunger pandemic' amid threats of coronavirus, economic downturn, notes, "An additional 130 million people could be on the brink of starvation by the end of 2020 as a result of the outbreak and its economic ramifications."[25] According to the UN food agency, the working poor suffer the most "as a result of the decline in tourism and exports, collapse of oil prices and any declines to foreign aid. The resulting death toll could outpace that of the coronavirus with 300,000 people dying due to starvation every day over a three-month period."

The pandemic is leading to a restructuring of the global economy, with an outcome that remains uncertain. Due to its extraordinary mishandling of the pandemic, the US experienced an economic collapse, with 50 million people losing their jobs. Many of those jobs will not be coming back. This has unleashed suffering and desperation on a level not known in the US since the Great Depression. European countries guaranteed salaries for their

---

[25] "U.N. warns of 'hunger pandemic' amid threats of coronavirus, economic downturn: An additional 130 million people could be on the brink of starvation by the end of 2020 as a result of the outbreak and its economic ramifications;" by Linda Givetash; *CNBC*; April 22, 2020

workers during the lock down, protecting their jobs. The US offered no security for its workers, engaging in a social experiment on a large scale.

At the same time, the stock market, de-linked from the real world of goods and services, was not negatively impacted but continued to rise. Massive amounts of money were pumped into the financial system by Central Banks and the Federal Reserve. This has led to an unprecedented increase in the global monetary supply, ensuring that the financial elite retain their bonuses and stock options.

The pandemic has also led to a "global education emergency," according to the UN. Unicef reports, "Over the past six months, about 1.5 billion children around the world have been told to stay home from school to help minimize transmission of the coronavirus. More than 30 percent of these students — around 463 million — were unable to gain access to remote learning opportunities when their schools closed." Social unrest, rebellions and riots are also increasing globally as a result of food shortages and immiseration.

The truth is that we require a systemic collapse or intentional "degrowth" of industrial civilization for humanity to survive at all. The continued expansion of industrial civilization is depleting and toxifying the Earth's ecosystems, while our intensive use of fossil fuels is leading to runaway warming, mass species extinction, the collapse of the Amazon rainforest, and the melting of the Arctic ice sheets. The best option would be a universally accepted strategy for a rapid deceleration and retraction of the global economy, reducing CO2 emissions, while we reinvent our technical support systems to harmonize with nature.

As I explored in *How Soon Is Now* (2017), we need to stop this runaway train and redirect humanity's creative and technical capacities. The alternative is to set, as a new collective goal, building a regenerative society where we mesh human activities with the biosphere, rather than continuing to exploit and desecrate the planet until we are driven extinct by cascading negative consequences. This would require a species-wide effort at limiting use of resources as we redesigned our technical infrastructure to support our future continuity.

The trajectory of the Neoliberal technocracy has been toward a managed, pacified society within an exploitative Capitalist framework that preserves the rights of billionaires, destroys the working class through automation and outsourcing, and supports the implementation of technologies of soft control. The Neoliberalism of Obama and Clinton increased corporate power and amplified a patriarchal form of globalization that excessively benefited the financial elite. This was sold to the people as the only alternative. As economist Richard Wolff has explored, Fascism makes its return when the failures of Capitalism become so glaring that a rebellion is possible. Workers must be sold a Fascistic, patriotic agenda so they will not unify around a socialist option, demanding a systemic reduction in wealth inequality.

The authoritarian Right removes the shock absorbers, laying the functioning of this unjust system bare for all to see. It also seeks to discard the traditional protection of human rights, human health, and freedom that was the underpinning of the Post War world formed at Bretton Woods, providing the ideological basis for institutions like the World Bank and the United Nations. Without this justification for governance, all that remains is naked power and control of the populace by force, amping up nationalism, xenophobia, and, in the US, delusional Libertarian ideals.

One can sympathize with the populist anger impelling the Qanon movement and the growth of the Far Right. The masses and multitudes are expressing an innate revulsion from the direction of civilization under the control of managerial elites like Clinton, Gates, Obama, and so on. They are looking for other options. Unfortunately, Trump and his cronies (a "transnational crime syndicate," according to journalist Sarah Kendzior, aligned with Russian oligarchs, CEOs of mercenary armies, and corrupt actors among the financial elite) do not offer a viable alternative.

9. THE PSYCHOPATH PROBLEM

As I write this, it seems likely that the US faces a contested election with a legitimate possibility of civil strife and mass violence. The media repetitively drums this message into the public. Right Wing militias are training for it. One senses this outcome is being stage-managed and orchestrated. Powerful factions, hidden behind the scenes, want to dissolve the rights and protections guaranteed in the Constitution. Our adversaries include China and Russia, who see America as its nemesis and have infiltrated our intelligence as well as hacking into our electronic voting system. It also includes the Far Right in the US, and the evangelical Right. These groups seek to establish despotic rule, authoritarian tyranny, ending the Democratic, liberal experiment.

So what is to be done? We need to develop and define a functional alternative. The alternative has to be so compelling, inspiring, and true that it leads the great multitude of humanity toward a new vision and a new opportunity. Such an alternative has to be designed to spread virally. It can work within the traditional political system, but also, essentially, build power outside of it.

Such a grassroots initiative can bring together the traditionally conservative working class and the liberal and progressive upper middle class together into one initiative. As unifying themes, this movement must focus on the psychopathology of the ruling elites, define a viable alternative to technocratic rule, and put forward a model of ecological stewardship. It must extend the social contract to guarantee people basic subsidence, continuous education, democratic participation, and social equity.

We can take a small degree of comfort from the fact that humanity has overcome past crises that seemed almost insurmountable, such as the two World Wars of the 20th Century. However, if we are honest with ourselves, we must admit that the scale of our current crisis absolutely dwarfs those of the historical past. We confront accelerated species extinction and ecosystem collapse. Humanity will not survive on Earth for much longer if we do not change our direction, quickly and radically. We are moving inexorably toward technological totalitarianism — either the softer, yet still invasive biological and ideological control system being orchestrated by technocrats like Bill Gates, or the harder control system that China is perfecting.

The accelerating power of technology has outpaced our ethical and moral development as a species. Unfortunately, conscienceless psychopaths control our political and corporate systems to a great degree. As Clinton Callahan writes in "Beware The Psychopath, My Son," civilization itself, based on pyramidical power structures, is largely the invention of psychopaths. It was designed to serve them: "All civilizations, our own included, have been built on slavery and mass murder. Psychopaths have played a disproportionate role in the development of civilization because they are hard-wired to lie, kill, cheat, steal, torture, manipulate, and generally inflict great suffering on other humans without feeling any remorse, in order to establish their own sense of security through domination."[26]

In his book *The Psychopath Epidemic*, Cameron Reilly writes, "The cultures of many of our largest organizations — business, political, military, law enforcement, and religious — attract and reward psychopaths. They prosper and rise into management positions, where they contribute to increasing the toxicity of the organizational culture. Combined, these toxic organizations pose an extraordinary danger to society."

The anthropologist Pierre Claustres found, in *Society Against the State*, that indigenous tribes in the Amazon and elsewhere designed intricate social systems to keep psychopathic chiefs or brutal Alpha Males from holding excessive power. This can work in small-scale tribal communities. As modern civilization developed to its present level of size and complexity, we lost the safeguards against psychopathic excesses.

Of course, the vast majority of people are not psychopaths. Most of us want to live decent, peaceful, honest, and honorable lives. Unfortunately, that will not be possible for any of us until we address our collective psychopath problem which now threatens to become a terminal disorder.

---

[26] "Beware the Psychopath, My Son;" by Clinton Callahan; *Possibility Management* (no date)

I consider it a severe error in the contemporary "spiritual" and "New Age" culture to not acknowledge the rule by psychopaths at the core of our deepening collective crisis. Nothing we can do internally, in terms of our inner spiritual work, is going to address this issue or change the outer situation. Those who believe that have been fooling themselves. But, then, what can be done?

The first step in reckoning with a problem is admitting you have one. The second step is learning everything you can about it. Then you can develop a strategy for overcoming it. "The psychopaths' only limitation is the participation of susceptible individuals within that given society," writes Callahan. It is estimated that true psychopaths are less than 1% of a given population, while those with lesser deviant traits make up another 5% of a population, and then a larger minority that can be persuaded to follow along. True psychopathy appears to have a genetic basis rather than being a result of psychological conditioning. Psychopaths are, in other words, a small minority.

Callahan writes, "Psychopaths learn to recognize each other in a crowd as early as childhood, and they develop an awareness of the existence of other individuals similar to themselves. They also become conscious of being of a different world from the majority of other people surrounding them." Psychopaths possess "special psychological knowledge of normal people. … They are experts in knowing how to push our buttons, to use our emotions against us. But beyond that, they even seem to have some sort of hypnotic power over us. When we begin to get caught up in the web of the psychopath, our ability to think deteriorates, gets muddied. They seem to cast some sort of spell over us. It is only later when we are no longer in their presence, out of their spell, that the clarity of thought returns and we find ourselves wondering how it was that we were unable to respond or counter what they were doing." This perfectly describes the collective cognitive condition of America at this point.

Psychopaths can be identified by brain scans: "When Robert Hare, a Canadian psychologist who spent his career studying psychopathy, did brain scans on psychopaths while showing them two sets of words, one set of neutral words with no emotional associations and a second set with emotionally charged words, while different areas of the brain lit up in the non-psychopathic control group, in the psychopaths, both sets were processed in the same area of the brain, the area that deals with language." We now possess the ability to identify psychopaths. In theory, we can establish rules and laws that keep them away from positions of power.

If we are going to reckon with our psychopath problem, we also have to study these character disorders, to discern their weak spots. Callahan notes that psychopaths "have little real conception of past or future, living entirely for their immediate needs and desires. Because of the barren quality of their inner life, they are often seeking new thrills, anything from feeling the power of manipulating others to engaging in illegal activities simply for the rush of adrenaline." This incapacity to care about or plan for a long-term future is a flaw in the psychopath's armor. It can be exploited, potentially, to defeat them. It explains why psychopathic leaders have such a total disinterest in climate change, the mass extinction of species, and other existential threats.

I hope this overview helps us understand what is happening on the world stage right now. As I discussed, the evidence strongly suggests that Coronavirus-19 was bio-engineered, probably accidentally released, but then knowingly distributed globally by the Chinese leadership. This is, obviously, a serious crime that should be investigated and prosecuted. But the mechanism for doing so doesn't exist. Similarly, Trump's incompetence and inattention allowed Covid-19 to wreak damage on the US population as well as the US economy. At the very least, he should have been removed from office for this, if not prosecuted. Xi Jinping and Trump are psychopaths addicted to the adrenaline rush they get from knowingly lying, causing harm, and subverting justice.

The mass media, over a number of decades, has prepared and in a sense "tenderized" the mass populace in the US for rule by psychopaths. The mass media is an instrument of mass hypnotism and indoctrination. Unfortunately, despite its extraordinary promise as a tool for liberating knowledge and connectivity, the Internet has been weaponized. It has become an invasive technology for social engineering and psychological manipulation.

Part of what enhances the cognitive dissonance we are experiencing is the tension between overlapping and competing agendas on the part of our deviant elites. There is an obvious tension between the technocratic managerial approach represented by the Clintons, Obama, Gates, Eric Schmidt, the Trilateral Commission, Davos, etc., and the crude Right Wing libertarianism / authoritarianism of Trump, and his minions, the Heritage Foundation, and so on. The technocratic approach is relatively sophisticated, while

Trump is crude and obvious. He enjoys boasting about his illegal and immoral activities and can't stop doing so.

It is difficult for establishment liberals to understand the appeal of Trump's childlike tirades and incoherent tantrums, which his tens of millions of followers still find refreshing. Across the spectrum, there has been a collective fascination with Trump as an entertainment spectacle. Incapable of controlling his own impulses, he speaks what was previously forbidden from a position of power. A Loki-like trickster, he has smashed apart the rhetorical and institutional structures that held America in a particular kind of psychological stasis, unleashing demonic forces from the unconscious. The Right Wing lower class appreciate Trump as an entertainer. He is seen as a kind of punk rock star/rebel who openly shreds conventions. This helps to explain why Trump is excused from behavior that other Presidents would have been crucified for.

10. CONCLUSION: WHAT CAN WE DO?

Let's rewind a bit, to clarify what we have discussed so far. A segment of the ruling elites in government, finance, and the corporate world are psychological deviants on the psychopathic spectrum. These individuals rise to power in hierarchical systems based on control, dominance, and exploitation. They win the game because they lack conscience. This allows them to ignore destructive consequences and "externalities." Psychopaths can sense each other and recognize their distance from ordinary human beings. As the winners of the power game, they see themselves as innately superior, "masters of the universe," who have a natural right to control and manipulate the mass population.

Some of them actively enjoy causing suffering. Over time, some of them get addicted to the adrenaline rush that comes from illicit, immoral, and criminal activity. Like addicts, they have to keep increasing the dose. As world leaders, they enjoy performing increasingly flagrant immoral and destruction actions without getting caught or punished.

This framing helps us reach a coherent understanding of events like 9/11, why the Chinese leadership decided to spread the Coronavirus globally once it was released, and the partly orchestrated social breakdown that is happening in the US right now. Psychopaths don't necessarily need to be meshed in tightly plotted conspiracies to be working toward the same goal and agenda. Their tendency will be to push societal forces in the direction that serves their perceived, short-term interests. They automatically project the barren quality of their inner lives into the outer world, reshaping the world in their image.

That we are being ruled and manipulated by psychopaths without conscience helps to explain the vacuous, numbing quality of contemporary existence. "When you understand the true nature of psychopathic influence, that it is conscienceless, emotionless, selfish, cold and calculating, and devoid of any moral or ethical standards, you are horrified, but at the same time, everything suddenly begins to make sense," Callahan writes. "Our society is ever more soulless because the people who lead it and who set the example are soulless — they literally have no conscience."

We can, therefore, define one new organizing pole for a global counter-movement: It will be based on identifying psychopaths — through brain scans, personality tests, and observation — and removing them from positions of power. This is something that people can agree with, from across the political spectrum. The various forms of psychopathy must be understood more widely, along with methods for identifying the manipulative mechanisms used by psychopaths to cover their tracks.

Along with this, we need to define a new direction for human society that is distinct from the technological control paradigm which is sociopathic in its essence. I believe that liberals and progressives are making a mistake in rejecting working class anger against automation and corporate globalization. They need to re-think their position, finding common cause with them. Similarly, I consider the mass movement questioning vaccinations and other advances in biotechnology and pharmaceuticals to be a healthy one that is worthy of support. The subject requires much deeper analysis as well as oversight from civil society.

There are legitimate reasons to be concerned that a rushed vaccine for Covid could have negative long-term health effects for many people. We have seen a massive increase in vaccinations since the mid-1980s. During that time, children have become more prone to many chronic diseases and conditions, from asthma to autism to ADHD. Vaccines provide enormous profits for pharmaceutical companies and billionaires like Gates. The pharmaceutical corporations that produce vaccines are part of the same market system that led cigarette companies to hide the danger of cigarette smoking and energy companies to disseminate climate change denial. Someone who develops a chronic condition is a long-term profit center for a pharmaceutical company. Such long-term conditions are actually advantageous to pharmaceutical companies, increasing their bottom line. Also, in the US, vaccine-makers have been released from legal liability for damages they cause.

My reason for writing this is to persuade those who still support the old progressive establishment or neoliberal agenda (which encompasses the technocratic / biosecurity worldview, the Blue Church etc) to abandon this obsolete ideology. We need to build a new alliance between the working class and the progressive "woke" elite — a group that includes those who have inherited wealth, plus the self-made entrepreneurs and tech company executives who flock to events like Burning Man, Nexus, and Summit — by defining a new orientation toward what is taking place as well as a shared vision for humanity's future. Before we can get there, establishment liberals and progressives must take a step back and reassess. They need to understand there are valid reasons that the masses feel scorn toward them, reject their ideal of progress, and are now embracing lurid and dangerous conspiracy theories.

People have good reason to freak out about ever-increasing corporate control and techno-surveillance, enforced vaccinations, as well as other aspect of the bio-security control agenda. It is good that they are rejecting neoliberalism and seeking alternative. There are, also, good reasons why many people deeply distrust the traditional media. For many decades, CNN and The New York Times and other mainstream news sources have been thoroughly infiltrated by intelligence operatives who shape the content and rhetoric of the mainstream news when necessary. We know this to be the case from many past examples, including recent ones, such as the media frenzy over Hilary's emails before the 2016 election, which tilted the election to Trump, or the laughable coverage over Jeffrey Epstein's "suicide."

Until space colonies on Mars open up, we still have to deal with this world and its fragile, increasingly

insecure and unstable realities. If we hope to change
the dynamics of the global geopolitical game, those
of us who wish to see a more just, ecologically sane,
and truly democratic society must coalesce around a
new strategy. At this point, no matter who is
"elected" as US President, this strategy must go
beyond traditional political means.

Much of our government and financial system is
controlled by psychological deviants, outliers, who
lack conscience. These psychopaths constantly seek
more wealth, power, and control, to compensate for
their innate insecurity and fear of discovery. They
recognize each other intuitively and work toward the
same basic goal: A destabilized and chaotic world
order that allows them to oppress, dominate, and
exploit.

We need to acknowledge the invisible, occult, and
ceremonial aspects of the culture, the operational
theater, of our ruling elites. Some of them are drawn
to secret societies. Some participate in rituals of
domination and pedophiliac sexual abuse which
directly express their position above and outside of
the law. Others share an ethos of self-interest, where
the "means justify the ends" (the ethos of The
Illuminati, an influential 18th Century secret society
which has become legendary) on an individual or
societal level.

When we turn our collective focus to address these
two issues — the psychopaths who have taken
control of human civilization and the technocratic
system that enhances their capacity to manipulate us
— we can build a global movement across classes,
races, religious and ethnic groups to defeat them. If
the mass populace's fury can be redirected and
channeled, transformed into a unifying force, we can

bring together various classes and political factions in a global rebellion against corporate and technocratic rule, in favor of local democracies and bioregional autonomy. We can focus on building a regenerative system that supports local communities and allows humanity to focus on our next great collective mission, that of healing the biosphere, which requires harmony across classes, races, nations, and religious groups.

ABOUT THE AUTHOR

Daniel Pinchbeck is *The New York Times* bestselling author of *Breaking Open the Head, 2012: The Return of Quetzalcoatl, How Soon Is Now, When Plants Dream* (with Sophia Rokhlin), and *The Occult Control System*. He hosts the Regenerative Futures course (www.regenerativefuture.net). His essays and articles have appeared in *The New York Times Magazine, Rolling Stone, Wired, Esquire*, and many publications. He consults with many companies and organizations. Join his mailing list at www.pinchbeck.io .